"In her usual straightforward, thoughtful, and passionate way, Enloe has reminded us about the importance of feminism to the study of war, violence, and peacebuilding in today's complex world. The twelve lessons she articulates concisely and clearly build on conversations, curiosities, and incisive analyses of war in different registers with different histories and inter/multi-disciplinary engagements. The thirteenth feminist lesson that she suggests accepts that new imaginings, speaking, and listening is tiring and needs stamina, but can continue with building feminist solidarities. This is a book for those who are concerned about the consequences of war and peace."

—SHIRIN M. RAI, Distinguished Research Professor, Department of Politics and International Studies, SOAS, University of London

Twelve Feminist Lessons of War

Cynthia Enloe

UNIVERSITY OF CALIFORNIA PRESS

The publisher and the University of California Press Foundation gratefully acknowledge the generous support of the Lawrence Grauman, Jr. Fund.

University of California Press
Oakland, California

Originally published in the English language in the UK by Footnote Press Limited.

Library of Congress Control Number: 2023938720

ISBN 978-0-520-39767-5 (pbk. : alk. paper)
ISBN 978-0-520-39768-2 (ebook)

Manufactured in the United States of America

32 31 30 29 28 27 26 25 24 23
10 9 8 7 6 5 4 3 2 1

Named in remembrance of

the onetime *Antioch Review* editor

and longtime Bay Area resident,

the Lawrence Grauman, Jr. Fund

supports books that address

a wide range of human rights,

free speech, and social justice issues.

Dedicated to Ukrainian feminists

CONTENTS

PREFACE

This Is Not a Girls' Guide to Waging Wars

WARS ARE LESSON FACTORIES. Out of every war – the Boer War, World War I, the Korean War, the Afghanistan War – come lessons. The lesson crafters are multiple: admirals, generals, journalists, politicians, historians and, of course, your uncle who pontificates over holiday dinner.

Napoleon famously warned that "armies travel on their stomachs," but then, invading Russia, seemed to forget his own war-waging lesson. Generals are routinely accused of disastrously applying the lessons of the last war to a later, different sort of war. Lessons, dismissed and applied, are the very stuff of military academy curriculums.

Some lessons of war appear impossible for war-wagers to absorb. Despite evidence to the contrary, they persist in believing that they can bomb the enemy into submission. Failures notwithstanding, many wartime strategists simply refuse to learn that torture produces unreliable information. "Beware the Greeks bearing gifts," Cassandra shouted, though the all-knowing Trojan men dismissed her as hysterical.

Other war-waging lessons have been turned into popular narratives. Often just a place name will conjure up an entire lesson. "Gallipoli," "the Somme," "Munich," "Dien Bien Phu," "Fallujah." Each evokes a lesson, usually a caveat about what *not* to do in war.

This book is different.

This is not a series of lessons to make us better military strategists. Rather, this is an effort to sharpen and deepen our feminist understandings of war. That is, what follows here are lessons in making reliable, useful – that is, feminist – sense of wars.

Absorbing these feminist lessons should make us more dependable allies of those women who are enduring wartime violence. It should enable us all to hold accountable those who abuse women in wartime. Embracing these lessons should better equip us to prevent and shorten wars. Putting into practice these feminist lessons should enable us to sustain peacetimes so that post-war societies can entrench gender and racial justice.

What follow here are lessons derived from scores of feminist thinkers from all over the world – activists, researchers and scholars from myriad fields. A few have been awarded Nobel prizes, but most of these feminist thinkers are scarcely known outside their local communities. Together, feminists – including many of you who are reading these pages – have observed, listened, weighed and wondered. As feminists, you've then puzzled again, kept listening, looked afresh at what has caused wars, how wars have been fought over years, how wars have been seemingly concluded and yet, dismayingly, how post-war eras have rolled on for generations.

At its core, feminism is about taking the lives and ideas of women – all sorts of women – seriously. *Seriously.* That means as if women mattered. As feminists, we together have learned that women and girls are always worth paying close attention to, not because they are always heroic or admirable. Though often they are. All sorts of women and girls are worth paying close, sustained attention to because they are *interesting,* they help us to understand how the world works and why.

Put negatively, if we do not pay serious attention to the complexities of diverse women's ideas and wartime experiences, we risk missing – or misunderstanding – the causes and consequences of wars. That is a risk that none of us can afford to take in today's fragile, interconnected world.

The twelve lessons to follow are ones that we, together, have learned from taking women's lives seriously. They are lessons grounded in the messy realities of vastly different women's lives. However, these are not "the" twelve lessons. These are twelve lessons ... and counting. There will be more. Feminists stay curious.

It has taken scores of feminists to keep my eyes open.

Ximena took me on a driving tour of Santiago to show me where Pinochet's military had set up torture chambers – in ordinary apartment houses, in suburban homes. Sister Soledad described the system around US navy bases that prostituted Filipinas. Insook opened my eyes to militarism inside a pro-democracy movement. Rela introduced me to the Haifa Women in Black. Ruri showed me the brightly neon-lit shopping area where the Tokyo Women in Black stood vigil every Friday night.

Ayse introduced me to Kurdish women in south-eastern Turkey who had opened a restaurant as a way to tackle domestic violence in a war zone. Madeleine tutored me in the UN's byzantine patriarchal ways. Nela took me on a walk up the steep hill overlooking Sarajevo so I could imagine the perches from which the snipers picked off civilians as they dashed out to run desperate errands during the Yugoslav War.

I have been lucky. So many women doing gender justice and peace activism and research have shared with me their experiences and what they have learned from those experiences. The twelve feminist lessons of war here flow directly from the grounded knowledge they have accumulated over decades.

I am happily in their debt.

ONE

Women's Wars Are Not
Men's Wars

SVITLANA WAS WEARING HER warmest parka. She had her iPhone securely tucked into her jeans pocket and a knapsack on her back, containing her Ukrainian passport, snacks, laptop, two chargers, tampons, extra sweaters for the children and the few family photos she could grab in haste as they fled. Her youngest child was holding tightly to her right hand. Thank goodness she was now old enough to walk. With her left hand, Svitlana pulled a roller bag filled with clothes for what might be weeks, possibly months, away. Her eight-year-old daughter, trying not to lose sight of her mother and little sister on the crowded Kyiv train platform, was carrying her brightly colored school bag. Svitlana's own mother wouldn't leave her own farming village. It was her home, she explained, even if Russian missiles were destroying its houses and silos. Instead, she insisted Svitlana should take her granddaughters to safety. Svitlana and her partner, her daughters' father, had said their rushed goodbyes outside the station, each avoiding mentioning her lost job or his deployment to the eastern front, reassuring each other they would phone and text daily. For now, Svitlana had become a single parent, a single wartime parent.

On a Warsaw train platform that same day, Agnieszka was working with volunteer women drivers. As Ukrainian refugee women had begun to pour into Poland, Agnieszka and other Polish feminists had become alarmed at the prospect of sex traffickers seizing on the chaotic conditions to masquerade as welcomers in order to abduct girls and women. Painfully aware of the shared conservative stance toward women by their own populist government and Catholic clergy, Polish feminists had quickly organized volunteer women drivers to provide safe transport to the frightened, exhausted Ukrainian women and their children soon to disembark from the trains.

Both women were trying to think, strategize and take action at the outbreak of a war. Their conditions were not identical, but both had to navigate complex gendered expectations with unequal gendered resources.

At the outbreak of the same war . . .

Alexandra had been too young to join Pussy Riot in their earlier outrageous public performances designed to challenge the Russian government's political alliance with the socially conservative Russian Orthodox clergy. But she had admired their courage. In the wake of the Putin regime's military invasion of Ukraine, Alexandra decided it was her turn to act. Bundled up in her winter coat, she joined others on the streets of St Petersburg in late February. She was politically cautious enough not to mention by name the man whose imperial dreams she opposed. She just held up her hand-painted sign: "No to War!" The security forces' brutal response to their peaceful demonstration shocked her. She dropped her sign and ran. Afterwards, talking privately with her twenty-something women friends, all of whom had come of age in post-Cold War Russia, she wondered aloud what kind of future her country held for her.

Lepa had survived her own violent war. A life-long resident of Belgrade, the 1990s bloody conflict had shattered her former country into ethnically charged, post-war Balkan autocratic states. With other local activists, Lepa had spent the Yugoslav War organizing a rape crisis center and feminist anti-war protests, defying the masculinized Serbian political elite's efforts to fuel popular militarized nationalism. When the latest regional conflagration erupted, Lepa's immediate response was to re-commit herself to feminist anti-militarism. But that was not the sentiment that she was hearing from some of her Ukrainian feminist colleagues. They told her that they wanted weapons, heavy weapons. Was sending artillery the new form of transnational feminist solidarity?

Alexandra and Lepa, living their gendered lives in wartime Russia and post-war Serbia, were determined to put the lessons they had learned from feminism to work in their own wartime activism. What that meant in practice for each woman was not immediately obvious.

Continents away, the same war was reshaping other women's lives . . .

Climate change had deepened the drought, making Evelyne's work all the more stressful. As a Kenyan staff member of a grassroots organization, she was working to empower rural Kenyan girls and women. Food insecurity was not an abstract concept to Evelyne. She witnessed how, even as women were chiefly responsible for supplying water and firewood and preparing food for their families, the conventional privileging of boys and men translated into fewer calories consumed by girls and women. Drought had only worsened those inequities. Now came the new shortages of imported grain on which Kenyans depended. Evelyne hadn't had much reason to think about Ukraine. When she thought about war, she thought about the conflicts in neighboring Somalia and Sudan, which for years had sent refugee women and their dependent children fleeing into Kenya. Today, though, she listened closely to the BBC reports explaining how the Russian military invasion of Ukraine was a principal cause of global grain shortages in African countries such as Kenya. Food insecurity, Evelyne knew, soon would become even more acute for rural girls and women.

At first, Lucile wasn't sure she should feel happy about landing a job with an arms manufacturer. Her nephew was in the army, but she never had been a military cheerleader. She did know, however, that, as an African American woman and single mother trying to make a decent living in Orlando, Florida, she should be pleased that she wasn't working in the region's Disney World-dominated tourist industry, where wages were low and racialized sexism rife. Still, did working for Raytheon match her personal values? Then the war in Ukraine began making headlines. Lucile started to feel pride in the weapons she was helping to produce: Javelin anti-tank missiles. She heard Javelins celebrated on the evening news. There was even a meme making the rounds on social media, "Saint Javelin," who looked a bit like the Madonna. Lucile wondered if being a skilled wiring technician in a factory producing Javelins connected her to Ukrainian women.

One war, intersecting countless women's lives, a global web of gendered politics.

∽

Most descriptions of war blot out complex gender dynamics: war is so bloody that gender doesn't matter. Or wartime strategic calculations are portrayed as so bloodless that gender politics are irrelevant.

There is a third wartime narrative. It features women. It is billed as "human interest," a story or a photograph intended to make a complex violent conflict – in Syria, Ethiopia, Myanmar, Ukraine – understandable to distracted viewers. The women featured are usually crying. They are crying over the dead body of a husband or son. Or they are standing stunned in front of rubble that was their home. Rarely are they portrayed as having full lives. Even more rarely are they interviewed and asked for their ideas about the war. Displaced women grieve over fallen men and lost homes. That is presumed to be the chief role for women in war. Their wartime feminine tears convey the editors' message. Too often, we, the viewers, absorb that simplistic message.

Feminists among us, however, have learned that in the midst of both massacres and elite strategizing, it is crucial to stay curious about the full range of women's gritty wartime lived realities. By "crucial," women's advocates mean that attentiveness to diverse women's lives and ideas is essential if we are to accurately understand the causes of war, the dynamics in waging war and the prolonged consequences of war.

Put more boldly, feminists from scores of countries, including our own, have taught us that if we don't pay careful attention to women, *all sorts of women*, we won't be realistic about war. We will mistake the causes of war; we will be superficial in our descriptions of how wars are waged – and we are bound to woefully undercount the true costs of war.

All three errors are dangerous. Perpetuating those errors makes the outbreak of a next war more likely.

∽

Becoming feminist in our attentiveness does not require us to claim that the politics of gender explain everything. Though, to be honest, on the darkest days the effects of militarized masculinities do seem to explain a lot of what is deadly, wasteful and unjust. In calmer moments, what feminists from scores of countries – that is, all of us together – have learned from each other is that when we pay serious attention to diverse women and girls, we are less likely to shrink them down into mere passive sobbing wartime victims or, just as risky, blow them up into unreal super-heroines.

Our collective feminist lesson: shrinking or inflating either women or ideas about femininity will make us dangerously unrealistic about war.

By staying attentive to the complex, multi-layered lives of women and girls, we are more likely to see how war-wagers strategically wield certain ideas about femininity – the "real woman," "the good woman", "the patriotic woman," "the fallen woman," "the traitorous woman" – in order to stoke militarism among both women and men. Stoking distorted ideas about femininities fuels and perpetuates wars.

By paying attention to all kinds of women, we begin to see men-as-men – in men's own class, sexual, racial and political (often rival) diversities. That awareness enables us to assess when and how distorted ideas about manliness – "the good buddy," "the warrior," "the fallen hero," "the coward," "the brilliant strategist," "the scientific genius" – are manipulated to promote and justify war.

∽

Women's wars are not men's wars. Start with marriage. Laws and practices of heterosexual marriage in most societies impose different roles during wartime: a husband is expected to act differently in a war than is his wife; in some societies, a husband is expected to leave his family and take up arms; under those same laws, his wife cannot sell property or travel without her husband's consent. Or take parenting. Women's wars are not men's wars because the laws and practices of parenting in most countries impose different roles: a mother is presumed to have greater responsibilities for children in wartime than does a father, even though she may need her husband's consent to take her children to safety.

Food and hunger are gendered even in patriarchal peacetime. It's not simply that in most households women are responsible for gathering food and cooking it for their families. Women also are expected not to eat as much as men in their households because it is men who are the chief income earners. Women in many societies eat last and consume fewer calories and nutritionally less protein. When wartime exacerbates food scarcity, the caloric inequalities between women and men widen.

Family structure shapes women's wars. Woman-headed households – conventionally defined as those households without an able-bodied, working-age adult male – are more likely to be poor than are households headed by an adult male. Thus, when thinking about women's wars, it is useful to know that, in 2020, on the brink of the Russian invasion, a remarkable 50% of households in Ukraine were woman-headed. That same year in Nigeria, 18% of households were headed by women; in Colombia, 36%; in Ethiopia, 22%.[1]

Women's wars are not the same as men's wars because it is women – and girls – who can become pregnant during any war. Currently, women in Ukraine have broad legal access to contraception and abortions. Just next door, however, Polish women's rights activists have mounted public demonstrations to protest their rightwing populist government expanding bans on abortions. Facing a disastrous drought on top of outbreak of civil war, women in Ethiopia in 2022 have won legal access to abortion, but in practice face limited reproductive healthcare in part because of the imposition of US foreign aid restrictions.[2]

Women's wars are not men's wars, moreover, because in most countries women's work – in factories, in services and, importantly, in farming – is more likely to be unpaid than men's work. If women do acquire paid jobs, their labor is valued less and paid less than men's work.[3]

During wartime, women are expected to take on added unpaid labor – to keep the farm going with fewer workers and less equipment, to care for children and elderly relatives, to feed the household despite food and fuel shortages. By contrast, men in wartime have to be paid for their work: even patriotic men won't fight for nothing. Weapons manufacturing expands to meet war-wagers' needs. Many weapons factories today are highly masculinized, though women can be found on the assembly line, especially in the wiring departments, or as clerical workers. For those women, well-paid jobs with Lockheed Martin, BAE, Raytheon, Mitsubishi or Saab can be tickets to economic security in peacetime.[4] During wartime women gain access to more paid jobs, as men are drawn from the civilian economy into fighting forces, however, it is usually presumed that they will hold those paid jobs only "for the duration," until the men come home to retake those jobs. "Women returning to the kitchen" is often taken to be a sign that peace has been re-established.

Similarly, in wartime, the sexual needs of men, married or unmarried, are often imagined to be different from the sexual needs of women, married or unmarried: it is a male soldier, not a female soldier, on leave after weeks deployed who is excused, even encouraged, by his male superiors when he seeks out a brothel full of women who may be trafficked from another disaster zone or are doing sex work by apparent "choice" in order to feed their children.

As feminists, we have learned always to explore the gendered politics of militarized prostitution.[5] It is likely that it will be the woman, not the man in her household, who is drawn or pushed into wartime prostitution (called "survival sex" by some humanitarian aid workers) to earn income. Then it will be her post-war social status that will be tainted if the word gets out about how she economically supported her children during the war. Her male client's masculinized social standing is likely to go unscathed.

Marriage, family, work, property, food, violence, sexuality, childcare, income, reproductive health, prostitution: each is shaped by gender politics during patriarchal peacetime. We know this.[6] What we may forget is that each of those political dynamics will continue when the guns begin firing and the missiles are launched. The gendered workings of these politics mean that women's wars are not men's wars.

∽

Our knowledge of women's wars tends to come from different sources than that of men's wars. It is men – especially men as fighters and men as senior civilian decision makers – who have had their experiences written about, turned into plays and films.

Soldiers' memoirs comprise a whole literary genre, though it is more likely that it is men from the country's dominant groups who have the incentive to tell their stories and to have their accounts published.

This is not to say that no women have written or made films about their experiences of war. Vera Brittain's memoir, *Testament of Youth*, gives us a gritty sense of what it was like to serve as a female nurse near the muddy front in World War I. Svetlana Alexievich's remarkable recounting of ordinary Russian women's grim experiences of World War II, *The Womanly Face of War,* helped her win the Nobel Prize for Literature, the first awarded to an oral historian. As a teenage girl, Svetlana Vasilyevna Katykhina, who served as a private in a Soviet field-and-laundry unit, told Alexievich:

We arrived. But they didn't give us rifles, they sent us to the cauldrons and tubs. The girls were all my age, loved and pampered in their families. I was an only child. But there we had to carry firewood, stoke the stoves. Then we took the ashes and used them in cauldrons instead of soap, because there was always a shortage of soap. The linen was dirty, full of lice. Bloody . . . In winter it was heavy with blood . . .[7]

Tran Thi Nga co-wrote her memoir, *Shallow Graves,* with an American woman colleague, Wendy Larsen, alternating their voices. During the

US-led war, Nga trained as a midwife and worked in hospitals dedicated to poor Vietnamese. Americans poured in money that fueled wartime corruption without aiding the most needy: "They gave lots of money to the man on top and did not watch down the line." Nga already had lived through the Japanese occupation, the war against the French and the war against the Americans. She could make comparisons:

> The Americans came to Vietnam
> and turned our country upside down
> with their money and their army.
>
> Their soldiers slept with our women.
> Their generals patted our generals on the heads
> As if they were children.[8]

Marjane Satrapi's boldly drawn black-and-white graphic memoir, the two-volume *Persepolis,* opens a window on to a middle-class Iranian girl's experience of the eight-year-long Iran-Iraq War.

> When we walked past the Bab-Levy's house, which was completely destroyed, I could feel that [my mother] was discreetly pulling me away. Something told me that the Baba-Levys had been at home. Something caught my attention.
>   I saw a turquoise bracelet. It was Neda's. Her aunt had given it to her for her fourteenth birthday . . .
>   The bracelet was still attached to . . .
>   I don't know what . . .
>   No scream in the world could have relieved my suffering and my anger . . .[9]

Some of the most engaging accounts of women's distinct experiences of war come to us as novels, often written reflectively years after the war they are describing. Ethiopian women's experiences of resisting Mussolini's 1935 military invasion are brought to life in Maaza Mengiste's twenty-first-century novel *The Shadow King.* After focusing on men's psychological wounds suffered during World War I, celebrated British novelist Pat Barker turned to the distant past to uncover women's experiences – and strategies for survival – during the mythologized Trojan Wars. After reading Barker's *The Silence of Girls* and its sequel, *The Women of Troy,* Homer will never sound the same again. Move over, Achilles.[10]

The rise of feminist historians in the 1970s and 1980s produced a veritable flood of fresh accounts of women's experiences of wars, past and recent. It has become possible, thanks to their innovative digging, to take account of women's experiences as wartime farmers, wartime prostitutes, wartime fighters, wartime refugees and wartime factory workers. Their historical research has made it less likely that we will slip into imagining that any war can be understood by merely focusing on "soldiers" and "civilians."

Jane Franklin, though the younger sister of the intellectually precocious Benjamin Franklin, was herself only semi-literate. She was a working-class daughter of Boston soap-makers. By the outbreak of the American colonists' war against the British occupiers, Jane Franklin was responsible for three generations of family members. In 1775, her city, Boston, was turned into a battlefield. Historian Jill Lepore, in *Book of Ages,* her innovative biography of Benjamin Franklin's sister, portrays Jane Franklin's flight from this warfront. She gives us a sense of what coping with war meant for a poor, barely literate city woman.

> Jane was among those who managed to escape. "I had got Pact up what I Expected to have liberty to carey out intending to seek my fortune with hundred others not knowing whither." She fled, first, to Cambridge . . . From Cambridge, Jane and her granddaughter made their way on roads filled with fugitives, to Providence . . .
> She fled from her home at the age of sixty-three, riding a cart through a city in turmoil, stowing her goods between sheets . . .[11]

Often, traumatized women in dire conditions are willing to speak to women researchers, if those women researchers have learned to avoid cultural stereotypes, listen carefully and fashion gender-sensitive, respectful ways of crafting their intrusive questions. In 2016, for instance, staff members of UNICEF's local office in Amman, Jordan, issued a report, on the extent, trends, causes and consequences of a major phenomenon among Syrians fleeing the brutal war in their country: underage girl marriages. UNICEF's researchers interviewed women and men who had become impoverished refugees in neighboring Jordan, among them was the mother of a Syrian child bride:

> No, I do not like early marriages, even though my daughters were married off at an early age simply because their father wanted it that way. I tried to stop him . . . but there was nothing I could do . . . I told him to wait until a better young suitor comes . . . but he refused . . . I really wished that they had completed their education . . . but our customs in the countryside are strict . . . and my girls accepted.

Because so many transnational organizations, such as UNICEF, UN Women, Oxfam, CARE, Refugees International, Human Rights Watch, International Alert, Doctors Without Borders, and Amnesty International have been influenced by the recent influx of feminist-conscious staff people, we are now able to read carefully researched accounts of diverse women's lives in war.

Among the systematic abuses of women in war these researchers have documented is sex trafficking by networks of local and foreign men, some of whom are serving as international peacekeepers. Women's rights researchers inside Human Rights Watch, for instance, detailed how sex trafficking operated in late 1990s Bosnia. They reported which young women were forcibly abducted – from Moldova, Romania and Ukraine – by masculinized syndicates to be bought and sold in Bosnia in the immediate aftermath of that war.

These independent investigators described what sexualized services these young women were compelled to perform, and to which men as paying clients. They detailed which men profited from this elaborate sex trafficking operation and which men in senior positions chose to turn a blind eye. They noted the few women contractors and women

UN officials who broke ranks and refused to shrug off the sex trafficking.

Human Rights Watch's damning 2002 report, *Hopes Betrayed*, interviewed victims, perpetrators and investigators:

> About a month ago, a lot of policemen came to the bar to celebrate the birth of a baby girl to one of the policemen. Since that man had already spent all of his money, Djordje [the bar owner and also a police officer] paid for him to have sex with J.K. [a woman trafficked into Republika Srpska] for half an hour.[12]

∽

A woman's war starts before any shots are fired. In those pre-war times, a woman's condition is created that will shape how she experiences war. A woman's war starts when, as a girl, she is taken out of primary school to care for her younger siblings, enabling her parents to pay for her brother's school fees, or helping her mother collect water from further and further away due to drought. A woman's war starts when her peacetime government passes a law setting a female's age of lawful marriage at thirteen. A woman's war starts when a judge dismisses her charges of wife battering as trivial.

As we have become more feminist in our curiosity, we have learned that, to make realistic sense of women's experiences of wars, we need to be curious about the conditions of women's and girls' lives before the war begins. We can't wait until war news catches our attention – in Somalia, Southern Sudan, Bosnia, south-east Turkey, Northern Ireland, Ukraine – to wonder about the lives of girls and women in those societies.

We need to pay attention to Nurtay Nurow, a Somali woman who with her husband had been a farmer. But Somalia's prolonged drought had turned their farmland to dust. Nurtay had already lost two of her children to starvation. She tried to save her third by walking miles, through armed checkpoints, to humanitarian aid, trying to keep her malnourished two-year-old daughter, Maryam, alive. She joined 165,000 Somalis in the refugee tent city. They too had seen the drought wither their crops, while the government waged war against extremist al-Shabaab male fighters who forcibly recruited children, dispatched suicide bombers and taxed struggling farmers. Drought, farming, war, mothering. They are each gendered. They each shape the other.[13]

Even if we are belated in our curiosity, though, we need to go back a week before the firing of guns made headlines and ask, for example, about the level of girls' and women's literacy prior to the outbreak of armed conflict, because taking on board women's and girls' ability to read and write – and count – will determine what tools those women and girls will be equipped with to cope with the spread of violence. For instance, a woman unable to read or write is a woman ill-equipped to comprehend the choices, even slim choices, she has in wartime. If her father, older son or husband can read and write, he is likely to impose his understanding of wartime choices on her, in the name of acting as her protector.

Similarly, if a pre-war government has set the legal "age of consent" for girls as low as thirteen (to convenience not only impoverished parents trying to cope with their poverty by marrying off a girl child, but also older men in search of a malleable wife), it is likely that the "gendered leverage gap" within their households will yawn wider. That gap will make it unlikely that girl-wives' voices will be taken seriously when family decisions are made regarding how to manage the encroaching wartime danger.

Moreover, if husbands' physical violence against their wives is brushed off by local police and judges during peacetime, to whom will those threatened women turn once officials prioritize war-waging tasks? When domestic wartime tensions escalate within families displaced or confined to shelters, to whom will an abused woman be able to turn?

There are still more pre-war conditions that will limit women's wartime choices and resources. In this sense, war starts for women when officials cut public childcare subsidies. The burdening of women with full-time childcare – and elder care – translates into women's limited access to paid work. When war breaks out those women in unpaid or part-time paid jobs will have limited access to money that she herself controls.

A woman's war starts when uncles and sons are given rights to the inheritance left by a deceased husband. It starts when women being paid less than men is widely assumed to be the "natural order of things."

A woman's war starts when a woman is deemed to be "alone"; if she is outside her home without a male escort. It starts when government officials assign land titles solely to male farmers. A woman's war starts when authorities argue that women campaigning for reproductive rights are violating the country's traditional culture, religious doctrine and family happiness – all three of which are what war-wagers claim they are fighting to defend.

∽

To understand that women's wars are not men's wars is not to adopt a hierarchy of wartime suffering between women and men. Because so many cultures imagine men to be the protectors of women, men are more likely to be conscripted into militaries. Because they comprise the great majority of militarized forces, more men than women die from direct wartime violence.

The patriarchal assumption that soldiers should be male, while it perpetuates society's privileging of certain forms of masculinity, does not automatically bestow benefits on actual men. In fact, it has been the patriarchally shrunken notions of male soldiers as strong, silent and brave that has made it so hard for many men to seek the mental health care they need to cope with the emotional traumas that come with soldiering.

Nonetheless, because in so many cultures women are imagined to be the "natural' caretakers of children, when women are turned into wartime refugees it is likely to be as single mothers with responsibilities for displaced, frightened children. Today, it is estimated that 70% of the world's refugees are women with their dependent children.

At the same time, because girls and women are the great majority of people whose bodies are sexually objectified, deemed the natural objects of "real men's" desire, while simultaneously they are imagined to be the property of fathers and husbands, men comprise the overwhelming majority of wartime prostitution clients and wartime rapists, while women and girls comprise the great majority of (though not all of) wartime's sex workers, trafficked prostitutes and rape victims. In other words, to absorb the reality that women do not experience war in the same ways that men do is not to set up women and men in rival hierarchies of suffering. Because decisions made by people – usually, though not solely, by men – that are based on their combined gender stereotypes, gender aspirations and gender values, women and girls, and boys and men are positioned differently in wartime. As a result, what they suffer is not the same. How those gendered sufferings shape post-war stories, myths, celebrations, and revenge narratives are not the same.

If women do appear in any war monument, they are most likely to be portrayed as nameless grievers or mythical goddesses of victory. That is, there is not just gendered difference, but gendered inequality in whose deaths, whose wounds, whose losses and whose achievements are officially counted. A uniformed male soldier wounded by shrapnel will be officially recognized. Civilian women wounded by shrapnel receive no ribbons. The male soldiers in a tank unit (armored units are among militaries' most masculinized units) which gains ground in combat will be publicly celebrated by the nation's leaders. Women who manage on their own to keep their children nourished amid acute wartime food shortages are less likely to be celebrated as the nation's defenders. They are just doing what mothers are expected to do.

Feminist lessons of war do not feature goddesses, grievers or super-heroines. Feminist lessons of war are drawn from paying serious attention to the wartime experiences of diverse, living, breathing, feeling, thinking, acting women.

TWO

Every War Is Fought in Gendered History

IMAGINE IF ALL WOMEN over twenty-one had had the right to vote in Germany, Austria, France and Britain in 1914.

Imagine if rape had been internationally recognized as a prosecutable war crime in 1992.

Imagine if most Afghan women had been literate in 2001.

Would World War I, the wars in Afghanistan and the nationalist wars in the former Yugoslavia still have wreaked their terrible destruction? Perhaps. But it is likely they would have been quite different wars. Women would have experienced each of those wars differently than they did. Those of us looking back at those wars would remember them – and be drawing lessons from them – quite differently.

History matters. History is gendered. Every war happens in gendered history.

Women's history is not men's history.

"War is hell." That familiar adage lures us into imagining that war is outside history. In fact, every war happens *in* history. Every war that we try to understand occurs at a particular moment in the histories of diverse women's relations to men, to the state and to each other.

Being aware of those gendered historically situated moments – in Poland, Colombia, Myanmar, Syria, Ukraine – sharpens our understanding of what women in any given violent conflict are experiencing, what resources they have or lack, what power corridors they have access to or are barred from. Being conscious of those historically specific gender conditions enables us to more effectively work in solidarity with women in that war zone.

⌒

In 2000, on the eve of the 2001 US-led military invasion of Afghanistan, a mere 15% of Afghan women could read and write. Afghan men's literacy rate was not high – though, at 47%, it was far higher than that of their female compatriots. On the brink of a war in which both women and men would have to scramble for information to survive, there was a 32% gender literacy gap, giving men a better chance to garner that necessary information.

Afghan women activists were acutely aware of this time-specific literacy gap. So they focused on radio. In Kabul, they pushed for women-focused radio programming. They scripted and aired programs designed to inform illiterate Afghan women, especially those in remote rural villages, about their rights, health and childcare. This war was being fought at a time of Afghan women activists' consciousness of both class inequalities, and urban/rural divides among women raised the political saliency of radio.

Radio has a gendered history in every country. So do postal systems, movies, television, mobile phones and the internet. In Afghanistan's wartime 2000s, radios were becoming common possessions even in poor villages. The doors to radio studios were being pried open by local Afghan women activists determined to narrow the wartime gaps between rural and urban women and between men's and women's access to information.

Yet, access to radio listening in wartime Afghanistan remained shaped by patriarchal assumptions and practices. Would the liberating programs scripted and aired by Afghan women in Kabul ever reach the ears of illiterate women in poor villages for whom they were designed?

Feminist media researcher Sarah Kamal decided to investigate. She found that, in 2004, in a remote Afghan village in the Samangan region, the radio indeed had become a prized household possession.

As such, however, it was controlled by the male head of household. The radio was kept on a high shelf, where women and children could not reach it. When the adult male took it off the shelf, only he touched the dial. Only he decided what was listened to. News programs were his preference. He took the radio outside the house and invited his male neighbors to come listen with him. Together, the men would learn about national and world news. Listening to the news added to their masculinized wartime expertise in the village and inside their families. Women within earshot could overhear snatches of the radio program, though they were expected to continue doing their domestic work. When the news program ended, the radio was returned to its high shelf. Radio programs on women's legal rights, on women's health, on childcare? These were not of interest to the adult men who controlled the radio.[14]

At the same time, in 2000, among Afghan girls and women over fifteen years of age, only 14% were engaged in work for which they were *paid*. This meant that for 86% of Afghan women, the devastating war would come when they did not have access to income of their own. Because women comprised just 15% of the country's total paid labor force, that also meant that their male fellow citizens – their brothers, uncles, fathers, husbands – made up 85% of Afghanistan's paid workers, earning income, even modest income, of their own.[15]

This would matter when the latest war broke out in Afghanistan in 2001. Money is historically gendered. Money matters in wartime. Who earns their own cash and who controls the money inside a family will shape who can make which wartime decisions for themselves and others. Over the next two decades, Afghan women pushed for their own access to paid work. By mid-2021, the proportion of Afghan women in paid jobs had more than doubled.[16]

Still, history is not synonymous with gender progress. Women's achievements can be rolled back by their patriarchal opponents. That is why feminists stay attentive. In Afghanistan, the progress in women gaining access to paid work was not sustained. By 2023, the proportion of Afghan women in paid employment was plummeting. Following the Taliban regaining power in August 2021, Afghan women were pushed out of most paid jobs, told by male officials to concentrate instead on their unpaid work in the domestic sphere.

∽

Americans should not have been surprised by this plummet in women's paid work after war. If they had been paying attention to the historical ups and downs of women's access to decently paid jobs, they would have remembered what had happened to so many of the American women who had gained industrial employment during World War II.

In the early 1940s, thousands of American women were hired into well-paid industrial jobs when the US government decided it needed to use women of all races to replace the civilian men whom they were drafting into the military. The icon "Rosie the Riveter," donning her red factory kerchief while confidently holding her industrial riveting gun, was created to represent this wartime phenomenon. But that was not the end of Rosie's story. The lesser-known American gendered wartime story is about Rosie losing her decently paid wartime industrial job when peace came in 1945.

When, in 1944, US officials looked ahead to men being demobilized from the military and expecting their wartime service to be rewarded with access to post-war civilian jobs, they orchestrated a campaign to persuade women to leave their paid wartime jobs, pushing them "back into the kitchen." And so was created the American patriarchal image of the white post-war suburban woman as happy mother and wife content with doing unpaid labor, depending on her employed husband for financial security.

For many African American women, post-World War II employment was chiefly in low-paid service jobs. Not surprisingly, the post-war white suburban American woman doing unpaid work is the woman for whom so many pro-Trump white "MAGA" enthusiasts today are nostalgic. It is this woman, who was mobilized into wartime industrial paid work, but only "for the duration", that they yearn. "Rosie" had access to a decently paid, skilled job only for as long as officials needed her there to help fight their war.[17]

To chart the workings of gendered history, we have to keep collecting data on women's and men's lives. An occasional snapshot is not enough. Feminists have pressed international organizations to regularly collect gender-specific ("gender-disaggregated") data precisely because, to get a realistic, historically specific grasp of the realities of wartime, we need to know how women and men each are living before a war wreaks havoc on their lives. Even household-level data collecting – still a favorite among some international agencies – drops a deceptive curtain over not only unequal radio listening, but also unequal control of income and unequal food consumption among women and men and boys and girls *inside* the same household.

∽

Radio, literacy and paid work are all gendered. Each rise and fall in the course of history. Tracking all three suggests the first of three ways that gendered history affects women's experiences of war: access to resources. However, to make full sense of women's wartime experiences, there are two additional historical stories that we need to keep following: women's organizing and feminist explanatory concepts.

Any war breaks out at a particular moment in women's local, national and transnational organizing and thinking.

When World War I ("The Great War") engulfed Europe in 1914, very few women in the principal combatant countries had the right to vote. German women could not vote, nor could Austrian, Hungarian or Serbian women. Nor could British, French, Italian or Belgian women. Swedish women already had successfully campaigned for their voting rights, but, on the eve of the war, neither Russian nor Icelandic women were allowed by their fellow male citizens to cast ballots. In 1914, Japanese women were barred from the ballot box, as were Korean and Chinese women.

New Zealand's women had successfully campaigned in the 1890s for their right to vote, but Australian women did not yet have federal voting rights. American women had been campaigning for the right to vote for two generations, but in 1914 it was a federal right still restricted to men, in practice to white men. Egyptian women suffragist activists had been organizing for a generation and so had women in the wider Ottoman Empire, yet, on the eve of a war that would reshape their lives, these women still faced stiff resistance from anti-suffrage forces.[18]

Not every woman denied the right to vote opposed war. Some vote-deprived women were nationalists, imperialists, convinced of their governments' justifications for waging war. Nonetheless, at the outset of World War I, when so many women were excluded from suffrage, some women did speak out against war – vocally, visibly. But even suffragists were divided among themselves: once the war began, would women actively support the all-male government's war efforts and prove to their skeptical male fellow citizens that women were worthy of full citizenship? Or, alternatively, would women plunging into war work simply serve to sustain the sort of militarized national cultures that had perpetuated male domination of public life for centuries? Famously, Sylvia Pankhurst split with her suffragette sister Christabel and mother, Emmeline, over precisely this question. Christabel and Emmeline threw themselves into war work. Sylvia remained a pacifist.

In the early 1900s both women and men living in societies colonized by the then-imperial powers – Britain, the US, France, Belgium, Portugal, Austria, the Netherlands, Denmark, Germany, the Ottoman Empire, China and Russia – were deprived of voting rights, even though thousands of them would be mobilized to do wartime work for those combatant colonial powers.

A generation later, in the 1930s, in what was both a post-war and a pre-war era, Swiss, French, Italian and Japanese women were still having to campaign to win the right to vote. None of them would have gained that right when the next world war broke out.

Similarly, in 1990, Kuwaiti women activists were pressing their male leaders for voting rights when the Iraqi military invaded their country and the Gulf War swept over their lives. Today, Saudi women are denied the vote while their autocratic government is waging a devastating war in neighboring Yemen.

Women's suffrage organizing is one of the success stories of the last century. More than ever before in human history, the promoters of war today must persuade women-as-voters that going to war is justified.

∽

Women's advocates never assumed that winning voting rights, as hard as that was, would guarantee the full array of rights. Other sorts of women's organizing would have to persist.

Many women activists have focused on rural women's lack of rights to land. Lacking formal title to the land makes a woman farmer especially vulnerable in wartime. At the outbreak of the wars in Colombia, Honduras and Rwanda, few women farmers held legal titles to the land they cultivated. Colombian, Honduran and Rwandan women activists organized to change this. In all three countries, these activists focused especially on women widowed by war, linking campaigns for widows and for women's rights to land titles. The very post-war survival of a woman widowed by war can depend on her having the right to inherit and keep access to the land formerly registered under only her husband's name.

Today, more women in all three countries have land titles than they did a generation ago, thanks to women's organizing. Rural women's land access, though, remains precarious. It is taking women's continued organizing in all three post-war countries to ensure that officials actually implement women's rights to land ownership.

Ending violence against women has been another galvanizing cause for women's organizing. Wartime makes that cause all the more salient. Women's capacity to escape a violent spouse can vary over decades depending on how many women-created shelters have been established and how successful women's campaigns have been in pressuring police and judges to treat men's violence against their female partners as a crime. Those successes, though, can be temporary. Women's past success in establishing court injunctions against violent men can be reversed when more patriarchally conservative parties replace progressive parties in power. This is the story in contemporary Turkey and Hungary, each now on a war footing.

A network of European feminist organizers pressed the Council of Europe to establish a Europe-wide treaty mechanism to prevent and combat violence against women. The Istanbul Convention is the result of this organizing. Continuous women's organizing, though, is the only guarantee of its implementation.[19]

The historically alert feminist stays attentive to women's organized efforts over years: before the war, over the months of warfare and during the prolonged post-war era. If we lapse into a short attention span, we undermine genuine feminist solidarity. Inattentiveness can lure us into a false sense of local women's sustainable achievement or, contrarily, it can produce a fatalistic discouragement when initial efforts fail. Neither does justice to local women's ongoing organizing efforts that will shape their ability to resist or cope with war.

∽

Side by side with gendered histories of women's access to resources and the gendered histories of women's organizing, is the gendered history of feminist ideas. Any war breaks out at a particular moment in the history of feminist thinking.

Three of us were sitting on stage during a conference in Buffalo, New York. We had been brought together by the African American sociologist Brenda Moore to share our ideas about women and wars. There was Lepa Mladjenovic, a feminist activist from Belgrade, Rhonda Copelon, a feminist law professor from New York, and me. Lepa and Rhonda were the featured speakers.

A member of the audience asked, "What about systematic wartime rape?"

Lepa turned to Rhonda: "I think it was you who first used that phrase."

Rhonda: "No, I'm sure it was you."

No feminist concept comes out of the blue. It is created in real time, in a swirl of specific events, by actual people trying to make better sense of a confusing world. A gender concept is created to shed light on women's and men's gendered realities. If it works, it should enhance women's and men's intellectual tool kits.

26

A feminist concept – in this instance, "systematic wartime rape" – becomes useful to diverse women only when it clarifies what is really going on. To leave events and relationships portrayed as a mere muddle, as if they were random, vague, or idiosyncratic (the proverbial rotten apple in a barrel of otherwise healthy apples) is to risk not seeing the pattern that is driving both cause and effect. To leave a pattern uniden-tified is to perpetuate impunity.

"Domestic violence," "Sexual harassment," "glass ceiling," "glass cliff," "marital rape," "date rape," "intersectionality," "double day," "homophobia," "femicide," "ethnic cleansing," "toxic masculinity," "gender-based violence," "women's rights", "coercive control", "survival sex" . . . each of these is a feminist concept. Each has its own history. Each was crafted by particular women in real time, amidst an array of events, often during an era of escalating violence. None of these concepts existed at the outset of World War II. Most of them weren't available in women's intellectual tool kits during the Korean War or the Nigerian Civil War or the US-Vietnam War.

To be useful, a concept needs to be constantly tested against the messy realities it is intended to clarify. When the concept doesn't measure up – when it fails to make more accurately understandable what it purports to describe and explain – it needs to be refined, sometimes even cast aside for a new, more clarifying concept, which, in turn, needs to be regularly tested.

There on stage that wintry afternoon, Lepa and Rhonda each credited the other with initiating this new concept – "systematic wartime rape" – that they hoped would better explain how wars are waged. They were motivated to craft this concept because, together, they were so deeply involved in the 1990s Yugoslav War. It was a war marked by widespread sexual assaults by men on civilian women. Lepa was a co-founder both of Belgrade's Rape Crisis Center and the daring anti-war Belgrade Women in Black. Rhonda was a pathbreaking professor of women in international law at the City University of New York. What they shared was a determination to not allow men's rapes of women during the Yugoslav War to be treated as those masculinized acts of violence had so often been treated in earlier wars: as the inevitable (thus politically uninteresting) "collateral damage" of war.

That is why Lepa and Rhonda had inserted the word "systematic" into their phrase "systematic wartime rape." Inserting "systematic" was a radical feminist move.

By calling the widespread sexual assaults by male fighters upon civilian women "*systematic* wartime rape," these feminists were asserting that, more often than officially acknowledged, wartime rapes of women by men were *deliberate, calculated, intentional.* That is, men's sexual assaults on women during war were not merely (uninterestingly) what goes on in "the chaos of war." Men's sexual assaults of women during war, moreover, were not (apolitically) just "boys being boys."

With this new concept, Lepa and Rhonda – a grassroots feminist activist surviving in a war zone, and a feminist professor of law an ocean away – along with their feminist allies were challenging the common patriarchal understanding of how wars are fought. A pillar of that misleading patriarchal narrative of war has been an assumption: what happens to women in war is not interesting, not political, not subject to public accountability and does not need to be taken seriously by experts on war.

"Systematic wartime rape" is a concept that challenges all four of these patriarchal wartime assumptions.

At almost the same time – the mid-1990s – in the sub-Saharan former Belgian colony of Rwanda, local women reporters and humanitarian aid workers were noticing an alarming pattern: organized, ethnically motivated genocidal violence by Hutuist (that is, not just of Hutu ethnicity, but proponents of Hutu domination) leaders against their Tutsi fellow citizens was accompanied by mass rapes by Hutuist men of both ethnic Tutsi women and those Hutu women married to Tutsi men. The first detailed account of Hutuist men's sexual assaults on women was published by the feminist human rights lawyer Binaifer Nowrojee, writing for the organization Human Rights Watch (HRW). Human Rights Watch itself has a gendered history. By the 1990s, as a result of organizing by women inside the group, HRW was taking seriously (that is, investing resources in) investigations of the violations of women's rights.

The fact that Nowrojee's revelations came a full eighteen months after the Rwandan War is telling. While the 1994 genocidal violence was going on, global media coverage scarcely mentioned rape. The sheer horror of the ethnically motivated mass murders seemed to drive all other forms of violence off the page.

Nowrojee's 1996 HRW report, *Shattered Lives*, was hard to read. It should be hard to read. Her interviews with Rwandan women survivors made it clear that the men who raped them saw their assaults as integral to their genocidal campaign. These Rwandan women's male assailants were wielding "rape as a weapon of war." They were not, as generations of observers had imagined, merely "boys being boys."

What happened in 1994 Rwanda was systematic wartime rape:

Elizabeth was twenty-nine years old and living in Kigali with her husband when the killing began. The militia came to their house while they were eating dinner with a group of people. She said:

"About ten of them came. They picked two of the women in the group: a twenty-five-year-old and a thirty-year-old and then gang-raped them. When they finished, they cut them with knives all over while the other Interahamwe [Hutuist militiamen] watched. Then they took the food from the table and stuffed it into their vaginas. The women died. They were left dead with their legs spread apart. My husband tried to put their legs together before we were told to get out of the house, and to leave the children behind. They killed two of our children. My husband begged them not to kill us, saying that he did not have any money on him, but that he had shoes and second-hand clothes that he sells at the market. He gave them all the clothes. Then, one Interahamwe said, 'You Tutsi women are very sweet, so we have to kill the man and take you.'"[20]

During the 1990s, attention to scores of conflicts, past and current, spawned related new concepts that feminists crafted to clarify how integral men's sexual violence against women has been to the strategy for waging wars.

On August 14, 1991, an elderly South Korean woman, Kim Hak-sun, became the first woman to publicly describe her World War II experience of being forcibly turned into a prostitute by the Japanese Imperial Army to serve in its Pacific-wide "comfort women" brothel system.

Feminist activists and women scholars in 1990s Korea, the Philippines, Taiwan, Indonesia and Singapore, two generations younger than the so-called "comfort women," supported Kim Hak-sun and other women, now in their seventies, who began to tell of their wartime experiences as forced prostitutes. In 2000, feminist international lawyers joined with them to conduct a formal Women's International War Crimes Tribunal in Tokyo, calling for the Japanese state to be held accountable for having created the wartime comfort women system. As one of the tribunal judges, British feminist law professor Christine Chinkin, recalls, the elderly women from across Asia who appeared as witnesses before the tribunal were breaking "fifty years of silence in which they had suffered isolation, shame, in many cases extreme poverty, and often physical and mental ill health."[21]

Feminists, nonetheless, began to question their own continued use of the Japanese Imperial Army's term "comfort women" to describe what these women had been forced to become. They decided that they should use a more accurate concept: "sex slaves."

This new concept – sex slaves – would prove useful in making more realistic sense of later conflicts, when women's rights activists of the early 2000s began charging other militarized men, for instance, in the civil wars of Liberia, Sierra Leone, Uganda, Ethiopia, with forcing civilian women to become the so-called "wives" of male fighters. Wielding their new concept, these activists pulled back this patriarchally camouflaged marriage curtain to call this wartime practice what it was: sexual slavery.

∽

Previous twentieth-century wars – World Wars I and II, the Chinese Revolution, the Korean War, wars in Spain, Burma, Malaysia, the Philippines, Indonesia, Bangladesh, Algeria, Angola, Mozambique,

Guinea Bissau, Rhodesia, Cambodia, Laos, Vietnam, Cuba, Nicaragua, El Salvador, Guatemala, as well as the Iran-Iraq War – were waged, discussed and researched without the insights offered by these three new feminist concepts: systematic wartime rape, rape as a weapon of war and sexual slavery.

That is not to say that intentional male sexual violence against women and girls did not characterize any of these previous wars. It did, though not always in identical ways or to the same extent. Occasionally, rape even became a salient topic of public discussion during or following a war. Often, though, it became notable only in the narrow political discourses of men blaming rival men for the wartime sexual abuse of "their" women. That sort of salience did nothing – does nothing – to enhance the rights or well-being of women. That masculinized blaming discourse has only fueled future revenge-inspired warmongering.

By contrast, what the introduction of the new feminist concepts of war has done is to treat women as full persons. Women don't "belong" to anyone. Some man's honor is not what is injured by men's wartime rape of "his" woman. Women who have endured sexual violence in war are citizens in their own right; they are humans deserving reparations, justice and political voice.

These feminist concepts also turn up the lights on war waging itself, blowing away the fog, breaking the silences. "Systematic wartime rape" and its companions "rape as a weapon of war" and "sexual slavery" have enabled us to see war more accurately *for what it is.*

In other words, any given war is waged at a particular moment in the ongoing history of feminist thinking. It's as if each war were waged at a particular moment in the ongoing development of eyeglasses. As we learn to grind more refined feminist lenses, we see the complex gendered realities of war more clearly. We begin to see patterns where once we saw only chaos or bad apples. We start to see decision makers and calculations where once we saw merely "unavoidable consequences" and "collateral damage."

Adopting new feminist concepts also makes us more curious about previous wars. Wearing these recently crafted lenses, we can look back with more acute feminist attentiveness to how both the lives of women and local ideas of femininity and masculinity were manipulated in those earlier wars. Suddenly, World War I looks different. So does the Ottoman genocide of Armenians. So does the Bangladesh war of secession. So too do the French and US wars in Vietnam.

Tracking the introduction and use of feminist concepts is one way to stay alert to the historically specific context of any war: was that war waged before or after we stopped treating sexual violence against women as merely "collateral damage"?

Today, exciting new research is being done by feminist historians and historically curious feminist investigators on earlier wars precisely because they are now equipped with these clearer feminist lenses. We can re-think the past in ways that make women's wars more visible.

∽

War *is* hell.

War is a *gendered* hell.

War is a gendered hell in ongoing *gendered history*.

THREE

Getting Men to Fight
Isn't So Easy

AT THE OUTSET OF the war in Ukraine, it was thousands of women with their dependent children who were fleeing, while men stayed behind to defend the country against the Russian military invasion. By contrast, seven months later, when Vladimir Putin announced that he was calling for a massive male military call-up, it was thousands of Russian men who were fleeing across borders, leaving women behind.

The numbers fleeing Putin's expanded military draft were estimated in the hundreds of thousands. However, not all Russian men of military draft age were sufficiently distrustful of the Russian state or possessed the resources to flee to Turkey, Georgia, Armenia or Kazakhstan: men in impoverished Siberian villages, men without marketable skills, men lacking the sorts of information necessary to make it across borders.[22]

Those Russian men fleeing military service remind us that joining a military isn't seen by all men as their ticket to unassailable manliness.

A month after Putin's call-up, Russia's defense minister was shown on state television personally reassuring President Putin that his officials had met the target of 300,000 new male conscripts, 82,000 of whom had already been sent to the front.

Less clear was what sort of training and equipment these new male conscripts were being given before being sent to bolster Russian front lines in eastern and south-eastern Ukraine. Referring to the newly mobilized Russian men being rapidly deployed to the front, one Ukrainian regional governor made a grim prediction: "The average 'shelf life' of mobilized personnel is two weeks."[23]

Militarized masculinities, as is true of all sorts of ideas and practices of femininity, are played out in particular moments in history. Most government officials have certain past wars they would just as soon their fellow citizens forgot: the French wars in Algeria and Indochina, the US wars in Vietnam and Afghanistan, the British war in Kenya, the Dutch peacekeeping deployment to Bosnia.

There is a reason, therefore, why Vladimir Putin has tried to keep his citizens focused on the Soviet military's victory in World War II. In the decades since that victory, the Russian military service has proved unappealing to many Russian young men. Corruption and hazing within the ranks have undermined both soldiers' morale and the army's reputation. The 1980s Soviet War in Afghanistan ended in a humiliating withdrawal. The two wars fought by the post-Soviet military in the 1990s against separatists in Chechnya not only left Chechnya's capital, Grozny, in ruins, but alienated many of the Russian male conscripts who were sent to put down the rebellion.[24]

More recently, even before Putin's expanded call-up, the Russian military was showing signs of personnel strain. By the end of month six of Russia's aggressive war in Ukraine, the forces that the government was relying on was strikingly motley. At the time of the February invasion, male conscripts were a mere 30% of all Russian military personnel. A majority of active-duty soldiers were paid volunteers, what Russians call "contract" personnel. Russian women volunteer soldiers were an estimated 10% of the military's personnel. Chechnya's provincial strongman, a Putin loyalist, took upon himself the task of mobilizing special Chechen male army units for the Ukraine operation. It is not clear how independently they operate in the Russian assault.

During the war's first year there were also male soldiers fighting for Russia in Ukraine who were hired employees of the Wagner Group, a private army owned by Yevgeny Prigozhin, a businessman reputedly close to Putin. By the end of the first eleven months of the war, the Wagner Group was reported to have hired over 35,000 men directly out of Russian prisons, promising them not only a paycheck, but pardons and social redemption. If they died in Ukraine, the Wagner Group promised these men an honorable burial, even though many of these criminally convicted men were pariahs in their home villages. Many of these former inmates were organized by the Wagner Group into inmate fighting units deployed to the front lines. These were the Russian units that suffered among the highest rates of death and injury.

How are certain men turned into "cannon fodder"? No person *is* cannon fodder. Each has to be *turned into* cannon fodder – by someone else. In other words, a hierarchy among militarized men has to be created by someone – usually more powerful men. Moguls at the top, cannon fodder at the bottom. The Russian male convicts – in prison for burglary, car theft, marijuana possession, illegal logging – were deemed by Russian military commanders (Wagner officers and regular Russian military officers) to be so worthless that they could be ordered to join frontline waves of scarcely armed infantry to run toward Ukrainian fire without concern for their deaths or injuries. That is, these male convicts-turned-soldiers could be used by commanders for their own tactical purposes – to exhaust Ukrainian soldiers enough to allow more professional Russian soldiers to follow in their wake and gain a yard of territory – without worrying that anyone would care about whether these expendable men died or were wounded.

To be turned into cannon fodder is to be turned into a militarized man, someone presumed to be without a wife or children or parents or friends to care. Men being turned into cannon fodder are not unaware of how commanders are treating them: some Russian low-ranking soldiers charged their superiors with reducing them to "meat." As one convict/soldier named Sergei explained, "We are prisoners, even if former prisoners . . . We are nobody and have no rights."[25]

Women relatives of these men, though, do exist. They are expected to take care of the men who survive being turned into cannon fodder. These women are on the receiving end when injured ex-convict-soldiers return home. What are these civilian women supposed to do with these former criminals-turned-mercenary veterans? Speaking of a twenty-two-year-old male relative, a former inmate-turned-Wagner-veteran, one woman said, "We all feel he is in some sort of hypnosis, like he is a different person . . . He is without emotions."[26]

Once the invasion of Ukraine got underway, there were reports of the Russian military paying men in Syria to travel to fight as mercenaries in Ukraine. It was a project that Syria's autocratic president, Bashar al-Assad, apparently agreed to out of his indebtedness to Putin and the Russian military for their decisive role in brutally putting down Syria's Arab Spring popular rebellion.

Progozhin himself, the Wagner Group founder, was once discreet about his private army. He became increasingly visible, however, as Putin's war ground on, making politically risky claims that his mercenaries were more effective in fighting the Ukrainians than were Russia's own Defense Ministry troops.[27] At the same time, his highly masculinized Wagner Group was a growing force conducting militarized Russian foreign policy in several of Africa's conflict-torn countries, such as Mali, Niger, Central African Republic and Burkina Faso, often replacing French military units. Women in those African countries now were having to deal with new masculinized military actors in their daily midst.[28]

Digging so deep into the proverbial weeds of one government's military personnel system may seem a bit excessive. Feminist investigators, though, love getting down into the weeds. That's where intersectional gender politics are often most telling. In making feminist sense of the war in Ukraine, then, it is worth noting all these different pieces of the Russian military personnel puzzle. Seen together, they strongly suggest that the Russian regime is relying on multiple militarized masculinities. Furthermore, it is likely that these diverse militarized masculinities are not interacting smoothly on the battlefield.

The sheer variety of sources of man- (and some woman)-power that the Russian government has been compelled to draw upon to wage its war of aggression strongly suggests that state military service has lost much of its masculinized appeal for most Russian men.[29]

Further complicating the government's aggressive invasion of Ukraine, at least some Russian men who earlier volunteered for, or willingly accepted conscription appear to have been dismayed at what they were ordered to do in the assault on Ukraine. In phone calls and social media messages to friends and family back home, male Russian soldiers expressed not only anger over their lack of materiel, but, more significantly, surprise at the gap between, on the one hand, their government's claims about their alleged "Greater Russia" Ukrainian compatriots and, on the other, the Ukrainian reality they encountered in the villages and towns they occupied. Where were all the Ukrainians who they had been assured would come out to greet them as liberators?

Military commanders in most countries worry about their male soldiers' "morale." In addition to assuring men that they will prove their manliness, have a chance to be heroes and fight for a worthy cause, commanders promise ordinary soldiers that they will have edible food, timely medical care and functioning weaponry.[30] Sometimes, worried that close scrutiny of soldiers' behavior will undermine morale, senior officers also ignore their soldiers' excessive drinking or their looting of civilians' chickens and motorbikes.

More often than they will admit, mid-level and senior officers, in the name of sustaining masculinized "morale," also encourage their male soldiers to visit brothels or to exchange food for sex with local women.

At a meeting of US military officers in Annapolis a few years ago, one officer after another came up to talk to me privately. I had just given a talk about military prostitution, prefacing it by saying I realized that this was not a topic most of the women and men in the room – admirals, generals, colonels, social scientists – were comfortable talking about. In confidential tones, each officer who later sought me out confessed, yes, they themselves had been complicit in allowing, even enabling, prostitution around US military bases or in navy port towns. Each expressed remorse. Yet each officer told me that they had little choice: men in the army and navy expected to have sexual access to local women as compensation for enduring the confinements and boredoms of routine military life. It was a matter, they explained, of morale.[31]

∽

Sometimes, however, commanders in the field, as well as the generals back at headquarters, become so desperate to show their civilian superiors and the general public their military successes on the battlefield, they push aside mounting evidence that their rank-and-file male soldiers' morale is plummeting.

By the sixth week of the war in Ukraine, for some Russian male soldiers deployed on the front lines in the eastern region it all seemed too much. Trying to prove their manliness was being replaced by trying to hold on to their humanity. In one unit occupying a Ukrainian town, Russian male soldiers got together and began writing letters to their commanders. Their handwritten letters were found, abandoned, just hours later when the Ukrainian military forced the soldier letter-writers into a chaotic retreat. In their letters, these Russian male soldiers pleaded with their superiors to give them relief from the horrors of war, to recognize the toll that their months of unrelenting fighting was taking. The Russian phrase they used to express their current state of desperation was translated as "moral exhaustion."

A young Russian-speaking Belarusian feminist taking part in a public forum in Stockholm in September 2022 explained. In recent years, she told us, "moral exhaustion" had become a common phrase among Russians. In other words, when writing their letters, these soldiers were not trying to be battlefront poets. They were expressing, in terms they believed their commanders and their fellow Russians could comprehend, the psychological depths to which they felt they had fallen. "Moral exhaustion" had come to mean "not being able to live as a human being."[32]

∽

Militaries around the world count on boys and young men absorbing society's double expectation. First, militaries count on them to internalize a need to prove their own manliness – both to themselves and to everyone else. To be seen as male and yet not sufficiently "manly" in the eyes of others, or even in one's own mind, is to risk being mocked, shunned, depressed or worse. Popular homophobia and the fear it instills in many young men have been gifts to military recruiters.

Second, militaries depend on enough boys and men – from those ethnic and racial communities the state officials deem "trustworthy" – believing that soldiering is a sure way to prove their manliness.[33] In most of our own societies today, the work force is built on gendered divisions of labor. Becoming a plumber, firefighter, physicist, surgeon or hedge fund manager can get a man over the challenging gender obstacle course to prove his manliness. But those masculinized career routes are selective. Most militaries, by contrast, are perpetually hungry for young men (and a few women). While the elite special forces units might pride themselves on being selective (and, not coincidentally, being hyper-masculinized), the infantry and the below-deck navy usually will accept any young man in reasonably good physical condition, especially if there is a war on.

"Become a man!" "Prove you're a man!" "Don't be a wimp!"

Militaries have plenty of civilian allies in fostering these gendered imperatives: fathers, grandfathers, mothers, prospective mothers-in-law, girlfriends, sports coaches, religious leaders and, of course, television and film script writers.

Even if a man is assigned to a desk job or the quartermaster corps – that is, to one of the military's hundreds of non-combat posts – simply donning the state's military uniform and being issued a gun will usually provide proof of a man's conventional manliness, sufficient to convince those men and women whom an insecure man imagines he needs to convince. How many proud parents and grandparents have a photo of their son or grandson in military uniform on prominent domestic display?

For those young men who, by the age of eighteen, already are confident in their own heterosexual manliness, joining the military still can have a double appeal. Soldiering can be a public confirmation of their masculinized assuredness. At the same time, soldiering can provide a chance to be a "first-class citizen," demonstrating patriotism in a way few civilians can match: "willing to die for my country."

This formula of weaving together militarized masculinity and militarized patriotism has had a powerful allure for millions of men and for many of the people who have raised them and loved them.

The success of that cross-generational global allure has entangled manliness and soldiering so tightly that it has been hard for many of us to see any daylight between the distinct strands. Sometimes, it seems as though "militarized masculinity" is natural, inevitable.

Nevertheless, not seeing the ways in which particular masculinities and particular forms of militarism become so knotted makes a privileged form of masculinity appear more dominant than it actually is. That presumption of the naturalness of militarized masculinity, feminists have come to believe, is dangerous – for most women and for many men.

Simultaneously, not being curious about the precise workings of militarization – tracking its ups and downs, its stumbles, its contradictions – makes militarization look more unstoppable than it actually is. In fact, an arsenal of cover-ups, white-washing, denial, contorted logic, false patriotism, heroic narratives, racist stereotyping, infusions of money, coercion and misogyny is needed for those who work to keep militaries supplied with men.

Yet, as formidable as those recruiting arsenals are, they still can be insufficient.

Paying feminist attention to military recruiters and drill sergeants is rewarding. These relatively low-ranking uniformed personnel rarely become heroic figures, but they are essential actors in tying the knot between masculinity and soldiering. It is they who persuade, entice, cajole, seduce and humiliate young men with the goal of getting them to pour their hopes for manliness into a khaki or navy-blue mold. If masculinity were inevitably, unstoppably militarized, there would be no need for recruiters or drill sergeants.[34]

∽

The wielding of masculinity to recruit and sustain a government's military requires the support of diverse women: women as mothers, wives and girlfriends.

Turning a spotlight on masculinities is not a new, hip way to return to the bad old days of being pre-occupied with men. Instead, observing and reflecting together, we've learned a feminist lesson: if we want to make reliable sense of the masculinization of soldiering, we need to pay sustained attention to women in male soldiers' lives.

A caveat: even if we forget to listen and think about the women as the mothers, wives or girlfriends of male soldiers, recruit-hungry defense strategists will be paying attention to those women for their own militarizing purposes.[35]

Women dating and marrying potential and current male soldiers make military planners nervous:

- What if a woman about to marry a man (or woman) who is considering enlisting decides that soldiering will not improve but jeopardize his well-being?
- What if a woman doesn't want to sacrifice her own career ambitions in order to lead the often peripatetic life of a military spouse?
- What if a woman married to a soldier riles against being treated according to her soldier-husband's rank (or, for lesbian spouses, the rank of their wives)?
- What if a woman persuades her soldier-husband (or soldier-wife) not to re-enlist?

Military personnel officials think about all of this – a lot. Yet they pay less attention to male partners of both female and gay male soldiers, seeming to assume that those men will find their own masculinized ways of avoiding the sacrifices that being a female military spouse usually entails. They try to persuade women already married to soldiers – especially soldiers who have moved up in the ranks – to socialize novice military wives, to show them how to accept and privately manage the stresses and expectations of militarized marriage. A thoroughly militarized military wife, a woman who has crafted her own skills at getting along in this peculiar life (for example, being a single mother much of the time) and who has come to appreciate the benefits that can accompany a militarized married life (especially for a woman married to an officer) – the housing, the healthcare, the community, the pension, the civilian admiration – is a military planner's best ally.

In most countries, women married to soldiers, even if discontented, stay quiet. Central to adapting to a militarized marriage is a woman's absorbing the notion that criticizing the government's foreign policy is tantamount to being disloyal to her own soldier-spouse. A thoughtful military wife may adamantly reject that dubious assumption and claim, instead, that she herself is not a soldier, that she is a civilian and a full citizen in her own right and should be able to voice her own views on political affairs. Nonetheless, in many societies today, her fellow civilians are sufficiently patriarchal and militarized that they may refuse to accept her claims of civilian autonomy, ridiculing her for her not "standing by her man."

Still, militarizing soldiers' marriages is never a sure thing. Women as military wives can experience domestic violence, shoddy housing, inadequate pay and pensions, their spouses' longer and longer overseas deployments, unfair divorce conditions, their husband's post-deployment mental health problems and, most worrisome of all, a deepening questioning of the very legitimacy of the wars to which their spouses are being deployed to fight.[36] Each of these experiences, if shared by enough military wives, can unravel the government's delicate strategic formula that keeps military wives on board.[37]

∽

Mothers. It is mothers about whom most military officials and their civilian superiors are most nervous. A woman who is a wife can be dismissed. Wives usually are. But mothers – they carry much more cultural weight.

If women as mothers of teenage young men or current male soldiers start to see the military abusing their sons, they are likely to speak out. No mother wants to see her son, the boy she has spent at least eighteen years raising, turned into cannon fodder.

Military strategists do not seek out women as mothers for policy advice, yet mothers make them anxious. Observers of Vladimir Putin's war maneuvers believe that he launched the war with the promise that no conscripts would be deployed to Ukraine precisely because he feared galvanizing Russian mothers of young sons. If he could keep those women lulled into thinking that only "contract" soldiers were being sent to the front, he was less likely to face civilian scrutiny for launching the invasion.

The fact that he later, in September 2022, threw that gendered caution to the winds and announced a nation-wide male conscript mobilization suggests perhaps how desperate he had become. He risked stirring up Russian mothers for the sake of stopping his military's retreat.

The Russian government is not alone in thinking about mothers. The US Defense Department concentrates much of its recruitment marketing on women as mothers. If one goes to the Pentagon's own website and scrolls down to their recruiting pages, one is likely to be struck by the attention devoted to mothers of young men. Fathers of young men garner much less attention; it is women as mothers who clearly worry the Pentagon. In both English and Spanish, the Pentagon's marketing staff try to persuade mothers of young men that the US military can be their parental partner in turning their boys into responsible adult men.

If you are a struggling single mother, if you are a mother of a son who is a school dropout or is in a dead-end, low-paying job or is unemployed, the military's "co-parenting" offer can be appealing.

Women as mothers, however, turn out to be not so easy to convince. In countries as different as Serbia, Nicaragua, the US and Russia, women who otherwise might not voice opinions about national security have taken to the streets to protest what they have seen as their state military's exploitive conscription or neglect of their sons.

Serbian women in 1991 took to the streets to protest the Milošević regime's conscription of their sons into his nationalist war. Nicaraguan women demonstrated against the call-up of their sons to wage war against the US-backed "Contras." US women – as both mothers and wives of soldiers – attracted media coverage when they criticized the Bush administration's failures to adequately equip soldiers deployed to Afghanistan. Impatient with the Pentagon's seeming neglect, these women – with journalists watching – used their own money to buy and mail Kevlar bulletproof vests to their underequipped sons and husbands in Afghanistan.

Today, many Russian women have decided that the military is neglecting young male conscripts. They are buying bulletproof vests, helmets, backpacks, bandages and sleeping bags online to give to their underequipped newly conscripted sons, husbands and brothers. According to Anastasia, a woman who is part of a group called Help for Soldiers, "From morning to evening, I scan the internet to find good deals for our boys."[38]

Patriarchal societies put women as mothers up on cultural pedestals – to be admired and emulated, though rarely to be listened to. The patriarchal men who run military affairs often confuse those maternal icons with actual women, women who think, learn, get angry and take action. They can react angrily when those mothers step down from their pedestals to confront them.

Consequently, Moscow's senior officials were caught off guard when women calling themselves the Committee of Soldiers' Mothers formed a network in 1989 to protest how their conscript sons were being treated by the military. This was at a time when political space was opening up for civil-society activism. Even so, most government officials do not want to be seen as attacking women performing their maternal duty.

The Soldiers' Mothers' initial public action was to expose the widespread practice of male-on-male hazing inside the military's ranks. The hazing was being tolerated by senior officers, the mothers claimed, and had become so brutal that some young men had committed suicide. The publicity the mothers garnered was embarrassing for the government. It challenged the very legitimacy of the military as national institution.

The women went further. They organized training sessions around the country to teach women strategies for keeping their sons out of the grasp of conscription officials.

By 1995, the Russian mothers were challenging not just the military's dysfunctional, abusive internal culture, but the government's national security policy. Specifically, they protested the deployment of their soldier-sons to suppress the provincial rebellion in Chechnya. Too many of their sons, they declared, were returning home dead or wounded. Suddenly there were media photos of Russian women commandeering trucks to travel to Chechnya to bring back their conscripted sons themselves.[39]

∽

Women who become politically vocal in their roles as mothers, wives, girlfriends and sisters of potential and actual soldiers are worth our feminist attention. First, their activism challenges the common notion that women are mere bystanders when governments go to war. Second, by taking seriously those women intimately involved in male soldiers' lives we can expose the lengths to which officials will go to raise and sustain their male-dominated armed forces. Finally, monitoring officials' attempts to co-opt and militarize civilian women – especially women as wives and mothers of male soldiers – enables us to see just how nervous even seemingly arrogant governments are about their own legitimacy.

∽

By month six of the Ukraine war, an estimated 70,000 Russian soldiers had been killed or wounded. Many men were listed as missing. After trying repeatedly to get information on their missing husbands and sons from the unresponsive Russian Ministry of Defense, some women undertook their own searches. They joined an online chat room called "A Group of Mobilized, Military Wives and Mothers." While they disagreed with each other, often fiercely, about the justification of Russia's war in Ukraine, they shared a sense that they could not depend on the military to care about their husbands and sons who had been sent to fight there.

This came at a gender-precarious moment in the Russian government's war waging. At the very moment when the Putin regime was heralding its new 2022 law criminalizing promotion of LGBTQ relationships because, allegedly, such relationships undermined the "traditional values" which the invasion of Ukraine was supposedly defending, the same regime was dismissing the worries of the fount of the most traditional value of all: motherhood.[40]

Belatedly, the Russian government announced that Putin would meet with a group of wives and mothers of soldiers. The women activists who had been responding to thousands of requests for aid from wives and mothers of recently called-up men were skeptical, even scornful. Would it be just a whitewashing show? No official had invited them.

One of the uninvited independent woman organizers, Olga Tsukanova, herself a mother of a conscripted son, dared the president on his own preferred ground, manliness: "Vladimir Vladimirovich [Putin], are you a man or what? . . . Do you have the courage to look us in the eye, not with hand-picked women and mothers in your pocket, but with real [women]?"[41]

As predicted, the handful of mothers invited to meet with the president were known for their vocal support of the war. They met around a long table, each provided with their own teapot. Putin told the hand-picked assembled mothers that they were fortunate that their sons were not dying in car accidents and not drinking themselves to death at home in Russia. According to a person in the room, Putin reassured one woman at the table whose son had died in Ukraine that she was fortunate: "Some people, are they living or not living? It's unclear. And how they die, from vodka or something else, it's also unclear . . . But your son lived, you understand? He reached his goal?"[42]

The Russian president continued to reassure the hand-picked mothers of soldiers by asserting that their soldiering sons were fighting a war against a corrupt and corrupting West: "They [the West] have a different cultural code . . . They count the genders by the dozens."[43]

Other women whose sons had died since the Ukrainian invasion seemed satisfied with the president's justifications and reassurances. An American journalist, Valerie Hopkins, traveled to the eastern Russian city of Ryazan in the tenth month of the war to talk to women there. She found that most of the women she spoke to, even those whose soldier-sons' graves they now tended, took pride in their sons' military service and solace in their having died for a worthy cause. While the women may have been influenced by the narratives offered by pro-war state media, it could also have been that Ryazan being the home of two military bases undergirded the region's collective faith in the military.[44]

Irina Christyakova was not among the women selected to meet with President Putin, nor did she live in a military base town. She told two *New York Times* journalists that she had traveled to the military's main morgue to continue her search for her missing conscripted son. She found a set of sprawling warehouses, holding thousands of photographs of dead Russian soldiers. She saw bloody uniforms discarded there; it smelled awful. Nonetheless, she was determined to find out what had happened to her baby-faced soldier son, Kirill.

She looked through hundreds of photographs. "If the face was charred beyond recognition, she would focus on whether the teeth resembled those of her son . . ." Irina Christyakova said she was no fan of either the Ukrainians or the Russian military, and she distrusted the West. Still . . .

"We don't give a damn about the politics . . . just give them back, give back their bodies."[45]

FOUR

Women as Soldiers Is
Not Liberation

THE MEN HAD FUN making up the list. It was 2022. They called it their "crush depth rape list." Sharing it among themselves, these British men serving as submariners in the Royal Navy imagined which women – women submariners with whom they were serving as crewmates – should be raped by them in case there was a catastrophe aboard their submarine.[46]

Submariners usually think of themselves – and are treated by their male superiors – as a special military breed. They are often handpicked to handle the peculiar stresses of underwater, close-quartered military operations. For most of the history of submarine warfare those selected to serve as submarine sailors have been male and from their country's dominant ethnic and racial groups.

Not surprisingly, submarine corps have been among the last military units to accept women. The Royal Navy lifted its ban on women serving on British submarines in 2011. By 2021, however, women serving on Royal Navy submarines still comprised a mere 1% of the total submarine service; 99% were men. The misogyny exposed among the British submariners testified to the ongoing resistance to compromising that masculinized exclusivist militarized culture.[47]

A Royal Navy woman sailor agreed to be interviewed on the popular BBC radio program *Woman's Hour*. She chose the pseudonym "Catherine." While serving on a British submarine, she said, sexual harassment by male shipmates was constant. A male supervisor once put his penis on her shoulder while she was typing. Stunned, she recalled wondering, "Do I say anything and make a big scene of it? Do I carry on [typing] and hope it goes away?" She tried to gain weight so that her male fellow submariners wouldn't find her attractive. The men's abusive behavior escalated. Then Catherine was raped. She did not report the assault. The culture aboard the ship, she explained, was, "Put up and shut up if you want your career."[48]

∽

English reformer Florence Nightingale and Afro-Caribbean humanitarian Mary Seacole are famous for showing the military how crucial women could be to waging war. Both during and after the mid-nineteenth-century Crimean War, Nightingale argued persuasively (over the heads of dismissive male army surgeons) that any military that could not effectively care for its male wounded would not be able to conduct its wars successfully. But these pioneering military nursing women – and those Black and white American women who soon followed in their footsteps during their country's civil war – were kept on the periphery of the military establishment. The men in charge of the militaries did not issue those women military uniforms and for decades refused to accord them military ranks.[49]

Taken together, the gendered histories of the exclusivist submarine corps and of the femininized nursing corps reveal the strategic formula adopted by so many male-led militaries: find ways to use women, but only in roles that military men and their legislative male allies deem patriarchally appropriate, while simultaneously pushing even those militarized women to the institutional margins.

The patriarchal goal has been to exploit women's contributions to war-waging, while jealously preserving the masculinized privileging of soldiers.

Waging a total war, such as World War II, motivated male officials to make typically patriarchal gendered divisions of labor more porous – women hired as bus conductors, women recruited as code breakers, women trained to be auto mechanics, women assigned to fly heavy transport planes. Yet those compromises were only conditional: "for the *duration*." This was the message of the Rosie the Riveter narrators, and it was a narrative that would be repeated when telling the stories of women in the military.

Britain's Royal Mail issued a series of postage stamps in 2022 entitled "Unsung Heroes: Women of World War II." There were sheets of stamps with matching postcards. One of the first-class stamps is titled "Pilots Meet in Their Ferry Pool Briefing Room." In the tiny black and white photograph all five women are in RAF uniforms, two wearing leather flying caps, one equipped with goggles. They are sorting out their upcoming wartime flight schedules.[50] We, today's stamp users, are supposed to be admiring, but not too curious. I wonder, though. Knowing what happened to "Rosie" and her wartime munitions factory workers, one needs to ask what became of these British uniformed women after the men in government no longer needed them. By 1950, what was each of them doing? Were any still in the RAF, any still piloting planes? I would like to know too what each of these women told their children, if they had any, or their nieces about why they were no longer pilots? It is likely that the British government counted on each of these women to shrink their wartime piloting down to a mere "adventure" along their longer feminized journey to marriage and motherhood.

∽

I used to collect military recruitment flyers. They were routinely on display in every US post office branch. The post office became a feminist field site. In the 1980s, after Congress, under pressure from American voters fed up with the Vietnam War, ended the all-male military draft, the recruitment flyers became especially interesting. While America's post-draft military recruiters needed more volunteers than ever, they had to make clear that only a few women need apply. My all-time favorite post office find was a four-page glossy flyer that listed all those military jobs from which women volunteers would be excluded: fighter pilot, tank corps, submarine corps, of course. But also carpenter and electrician. No woman should have gotten her hopes up that by enlisting in the US army she might acquire economically useful carpenters' or electricians' skills.

I tried to picture the meeting at the Pentagon during which people around the table decided that military carpenter and electrician should be kept as male preserves. Were those jobs imagined to be carried out too close to "combat"?

"Combat." Feminist activists, legislators and investigators who have spent years tracking sexism inside militaries have learned that "combat" should always be accompanied by quotation marks. That is, "combat" should never be treated as if it were an obvious job category. In reality, they have found, "combat" is contested and fluid. What is officially defined as "combat" expands and shrinks.[51]

Winston Churchill, desperate for "manpower" late in World War II, managed to smuggle women into British long-range artillery units as targeters, assuming that if these women weren't actually firing the heavy weapons, they weren't "combat" personnel. By 2000, the US Defense Department had revised their recruiting brochure. Carpenter and electrician were no longer considered "combat" jobs and thus were opened to women. Warfare hadn't changed. The gender politics had.

During the 1980s to 2000s, as women equality activists challenged their governments to dismantle the masculinized institutional fortresses of their state militaries, "combat" took on increased saliency. If women were going to be recruited in larger numbers, the defenders of militarized patriarchy schemed, then at least they should be kept out of "combat" posts. Alarmed, they saw preserve of true manliness shrinking. It used to include kitchen staff, supply managers and airplane mechanics. Now, genuine manliness could be proved only in an all-male infantry-forward position – inside a tank, in a fighter plane cockpit or under water in a submarine. Military decision makers turned themselves into pretzels in the name of preserving masculinized "combat."

By the 1990s, American campaigners who were pushing to open up this bastion of male privilege had several points on their side. Among their allies were women military officers who explained to members of legislatures that they were serious careerists, being stymied in their promotion to senior ranks because those senior posts were traditionally given only to officers who had had "combat" command experience. That excluded the most talented, committed career-women officers. On top of that, the advocates argued, modern warfare no longer had clear spatial distinctions between "front" and "rear." The spatial purity of "combat" was an outdated myth. This was driven home when thirteen US women soldiers – all assigned to allegedly "non-combat" posts – were killed in an attack during the 1991 Gulf War.[52]

By the early 2000s, many militaries, including most in NATO (the Dutch were the first), had done away with the male-only "combat" rule. This did not mean, however, that the contest over the masculinization of combat was over. Today, the newest arena for this ongoing tussle is militaries' special forces. Those units of a military – the US Navy Seals, the British SAS and their exclusivist counterparts – work the hardest to maintain their narrow, masculinized gateway.

Still, since the 1970s, scores of state militaries have opened their doors, at least a crack, to women – though most have accepted women only as volunteers. Among the few governments that now conscript women as well as men are Eritrea, Israel, Norway and Sweden.

Our understandings of women as soldiers (and sailors and pilots) remain in flux.

∾

In the 1990s and early 2000s, governments – under civil-society pressure and usually begrudgingly – lifted their bans on gay men and lesbians serving openly in the militaries. For decades, lesbians in militaries had experienced militarized homophobia more intensely than had even gay men. Lesbians in uniform not only violated society's conventional norms of femininity, they joined the military precisely in order to play roles that were designed to be the preserve of manly men, and they were uninterested in straight male soldiers' sexual advances. One reflection of the special pressures on lesbians was that, during the 1980s and 1990s, although women in the US military were less than one fifth of all active-duty personnel, they were dishonorably dismissed at higher levels than men for violating the US ban on gays and lesbians in the armed forces.[53]

Today, in the post-ban era, some militaries seem to be deliberately pursuing LGBTQ+ youth as volunteer enlistees. Where once these young people were imagined to be threats to military effectiveness, they now appear to be the ticket to recruiters filling their monthly quotas. For some young lesbians, LGBTQ-welcoming militaries provide opportunities that their own civilian hometowns and workplaces still do not afford.[54]

∽

In its simplest form, the feminist puzzle is this: are the increasing numbers of women joining state militaries evidence of male-dominated governments' clever co-optation of women into their militarized schemes? Alternatively, should we see the rising numbers of women joining militaries as one more feminist advance in dismantling patriarchy?

Feminists in scores of countries ask whether a woman soldier represents women's increasing militarization or a pathway to women's liberation.

In the early 1980s, a small transnational feminist workshop was held in Amsterdam to tease out this very puzzle. Most of the dozen or so women around the table had to be persuaded to attend. Traveling to the Netherlands – from Canada, Germany, Italy, the Netherlands itself, the US and Britain – to spend three days discussing women in militaries did not seem to these busy women's advocates a good use of their time. Women in militaries was way down their lists of issues, precisely because they assumed that opening doors to women in the military was just another step towards militarization. Even paying attention to women in militaries might compromise their own feminism.

One of the highlights of our gathering was going together to see the then-new Hollywood film *Private Benjamin*, starring Goldie Hawn. It had just opened in Amsterdam. The Europeans among us came out the theater stunned. Did American women really believe that the way for a woman to put her life back together after a divorce was to join the military?

By the end of our three days together, the table was cluttered with coffee mugs, breadcrumbs and orange peels. Still, we had found, much to our surprise, that, even as feminists wary of militarization, we shared questions to pursue, common developments to track. For instance, we realized that militaries in our several countries had quite different approaches – and motivations – for enlisting women: to compensate for lost male conscripts, to look "modern," to fill gaps in special job categories.

Listening to each other, we also began wondering why young women voluntarily enlisted. Were they delaying marriage, escaping a stifling small town, finding community with other women? Or were they trying to earn the respect of their militarized fathers, to have an adventure, to pursue opportunities not available for them in a racially discriminatory civilian labor market?

We could see that our own societies' particular histories of war generated quite dissimilar popular attitudes toward women as soldiers. Americans, despite having just come out of an alienating war in Vietnam, could still collectively indulge in a kind of militarized nostalgia derived from their experience of World War II, "the Good War." It was a nostalgia to which most Germans were collectively allergic. Furthermore, we became more sensitive to the differences between our own women's movements: British feminists in the 1980s were far closer to their class-based labor movement than were the Americans, for whom equality held such a strong appeal.[55]

Some of the differences that we discovered in those early conversations remain important today.

∽

Currently, women make up 30% or more of the Israeli and Eritrean militaries, both of which subject women, as well as men, to conscription.[56] At the same time, women are 19% of the Australian military, 16% of the US military, and 11% of the UK military, all of which have ended male conscription and instead recruit men and women as contract volunteers. In wartime Ukraine, women have climbed to 23% of soldiers; men are conscripted, women join as volunteers.

Looking at the current proportions of women in various militaries should motivate us to ask sharper questions – about militaries, wars, diverse women, distinct women's movements.

Women as percentage of state active-duty military forces in other selected countries, 2016 – 2020:

Canada – 16%
China – 7.5%
Fiji – 20%
France – 16%
Germany – 12 %
Hungary – 20%
India – 0.7%
Israel – 33 %
Japan – 8%
Poland – 7%
Russia – 10%
Sweden – 15%
South Africa – 24%
Taiwan – 15%
Turkey – 0.3%

Numbers can be numbing. Yet, if one looks at the proportions of women in the military of each country as a reflection of gender politics, the figures can be intriguing.[57]

For instance, two of the militaries with the highest proportions of women in uniform are serving dismayingly autocratic regimes: Hungary and Eritrea. Viktor Orbán's Hungarian regime is no friend of women's rights. He has aggressively pushed back against the very notion of gender equity and pressed women to forego their reproductive rights and to prioritize their domestic unpaid roles. Do the hundreds of women joining the Hungarian military, though seemingly going against this patriarchal vision of womanhood, nonetheless see themselves as defenders of that vision?

Eritrea's autocratic ruler, President Isaias Afwerki, imposed compulsory military service on both women and men, motivating many Eritreans to flee the country. Furthermore, his military has been accused of committing sexual abuses against ethnic Tigray women in neighboring Ethiopia, as it has joined the Ethiopian administration of President Abiy Ahmed in its brutal war against Tigray insurgents. What roles are Eritrean conscripted women assigned to in Isaias' military? We know far too little about what these uniformed Eritrean women think about their military service, about their government, or about their sexually abusive male soldier colleagues.[58]

The Turkish military stands out in this list as well. It has remained one of the world's most masculinized militaries, with 99.7% male soldiers. This is despite Turkey being a member of NATO, which, since the 1990s, has heralded itself as promoter of gender equality, urging member states to increase the recruitment of women into their ranks. Perhaps the Turkish government still having access to male conscripts has meant its defense officials haven't seen enlisting women to be necessary, even given their waging an extended war against Kurdish insurgents in its south-east. Then too, there is Turkey's increasingly autocratic rule under political leader President Erdoğan. His regime has become increasingly dependent upon a gender-conservative popular civilian voting base. Furthermore, it is rare to hear any Turkish feminist needing to prioritize other urgent issues, to raise women's equality within the military as a major issue.

Or consider Fiji. While apparently a minor player in global politics, Fiji's military politics has caused waves in the regional affairs of the South Pacific. On the eve of independence in 1970, Fiji was a starkly divided society, with 56% of its citizens ethnic Fijians and 35% ethnic Indo-Fijians. Fiji's military was created by Britain, when it was its colonial ruler, to be a source of employment and communal pride for ethnic Fijian men. Locally, an ethnicized, masculinized military was imagined by a patriarchal alliance of ethnic Fijian male chiefs and ethnic Fijian Methodist male clergy to be a pillar of the newly independent state.

When some Fijian women began to push for membership in this military, they were facing both an ethnicized and masculinized institution. Moreover, it was a military whose senior officers saw themselves as superior to the country's elected Fijian and Indian civilian officials. Between 1987 and 2006, the ethnic Fijian men at the top of the country's military performed four coups d'etat. This is the military some Fijian women sought to join, in the name of equal opportunity.

The late Teresia Teaiwa was the feminist researcher and activist who taught so many of us to take seriously women in Fiji's military.[59] Teresia was a critic of the militarizing trends she saw throughout the South Pacific. She wisely warned us, however, not to overlook these women simply because Fiji is not a great power or because Fiji's military has been so ethnically polarizing and anti-democratic. Rather, she said, her years of interviewing Fijian women from three distinct generations – a majority of them ethnic Fijians – revealed to her how these down-to-earth women calculated that becoming a soldier would secure their families' incomes and enhance their own personal social mobility. She described them as "pragmatic."

Afterall, Fiji has become a major contributor to UN peacekeeping operations – in Lebanon, Syria, South Sudan, Timor-Leste. And international peacekeeping duty pays well. Fijian young women today look out on the world pragmatically. Should they enlist in Fiji's state military, where they can earn extra pay as a peacekeeper? Or are their prospects improved if they sign up with one of the proliferating globalized private security companies that come to Suva in search of male and female recruits?

Women in the US military attract the most international attention because the US is a major player in world politics and women in the US garner disproportionate attention of globalized news and entertainment media. It was Goldie Hawn's *Private Benjamin* – not a Turkish or Fijian woman soldier – who was on that cinema screen in 1980s Amsterdam.

Looking at the long (though incomplete) list of numbers, one can see that the US military is not among those with the highest proportions of women in their current military ranks. The militaries of Eritrea, Israel, South Africa, Hungary and Australia have out-paced the US. Yet, looking at any military, one must move beyond the numbers to ask racial and ethnic questions.

A small meeting was held in the early 1990s in Washington to discuss race relations in the US military. These were the years when civil rights organizations, such as the NAACP, monitored the federal government; when the US military was trying to put its Vietnam war disasters behind it; when the military had to fill its ranks without the aid of male draft. Around the table were civil rights campaigners, Black sociologists, members of Congress, mid-level Defense Department officials, several uniformed active-duty personnel and a smattering of civilian researchers.

The discussion initially focused almost entirely on Black men in the US military – their promotion rates, their re-enlistment rates, their proportions of dishonorable discharges, their charges of discrimination – not because this was a meeting explicitly about men (and certainly not about masculinities), but because, for most of the participants, talking about "Blacks in the military" meant talking about Black men.[60]

There was a lull in the flow of conversation. Ed Dorn, an African American civil rights advocate and policy specialist, piped up: "You know, Black women are 48% of all enlisted women in the US Army." There was a stunned silence. Then the Congressman at the table – who would soon be named Secretary of Defense – looked at Ed and said something to the effect of, "That's not possible."

It didn't seem possible because almost no one at the table had given any thought to Black women joining the military. It was Black men who were the issue. No one had bothered to notice that Black women admired their aunts and mothers who had enlisted in earlier generations and had made their own calculations about their chances in a racialized civilian workplace.[61]

Today, Black women comprise 29% of all active-duty military women, yet make up only 12% of all women in American society. That active-duty percentage is down a bit from African American women's all-time high in the 1990s, but still more than twice what one might expect if there were no racialized gendered dynamics in American society or the military.

Simultaneously, over the past twenty years, Latinas, who comprise about 18% of all American women, have risen to 21% of all active-duty women in the US military.

Clearly two things are going on in any gendered, ethnicized, racialized military today. First, male-dominated policy elites are continuing to think of women in their militaries in terms of their own strategic needs: to compensate for losing male soldiers when male conscription ends; to look "modern" in the eyes of other international actors by enlisting at least a few women; to make compromises with their own local women's equality advocates; to worry less about women enlistees' racial or ethnic affiliations than about comparable male soldiers' identities.

Yet, second and simultaneously, women in societies as dissimilar as Fiji and the US are making their own assessments. Soldiering is not only an activity designed to strengthen the government's capacity for violence, it is, in the eyes of many young women, a job: a job with benefits, a job with social status.

Feminists have had to understand that women, especially young women of diverse communities and sexualities, have their own aspirations and make their own calculations. Women's advocates have had to couple that understanding with their political goal of not letting the military as an institution carry on in its masculinized, patriarchal ways. At the same time – here's the hard part – feminists have had to remain wary of treating the military as merely another job site, thus staying alert to the co-opting allures of militarism.

Anything can be militarized, feminists warn each other, even gender equality.

∾

How does a feminist think through male soldiers' sexual violence against women soldiers?

Three questions are being asked by feminists to make sense of this seeming epidemic. First, are sexually abusive military men using violence to signal to women that they do not belong in a privileged masculinized space? That is, whatever other motives these uniformed male perpetrators may have, part of what seems to be fueling their sexualized aggression is their resentment towards women for "invading" a space those men imagined they owned.

Second, feminists ask: what is behind the systematic refusal by so many senior male officers – and their civilian superiors – to take violence against women inside their militaries seriously? To get at the roots of sexual harassment and assault in any organization, we need to investigate the senior enablers.

An enabler is anyone who could pay attention and doesn't. An enabler is anyone who could intervene and chooses not to. The perpetrators of sexual violence are not the only story. So are the enablers.

Third, feminists investigating and campaigning against intra-military violence against women want to hear from the uniformed women who have been abused or intimidated by the threats of abuse. How should feminists go about listening to these women – of all ranks, of different sexual and racial identities – in order to devise the most effective and fair strategies of response?

Investigating militaries with questions flowing from #MeToo movements – in South Korea, India, Japan, Sweden, Mexico, Kenya, as well as the United Nations – reminds us that, while militaries may be distinct, they are *not* unique.

To think of any military as unique – as somehow so special it is immune from comparison with any other organization – puts one on a slippery slope toward presuming that only people with special skills, special access, special insider knowledge can understand and expose violence against women inside militaries. That presumption provides a military with a protective covering it does not deserve, a presumption that perpetuates militarization.

∽

The exposure of male soldiers' sexual violence against women comrades has been achieved by an alliance of insiders and outsiders, people in uniform and civilian allies: feminist activists, members of legislatures, journalists, independent researchers and women in uniform themselves.[62]

One of the first exposés to demonstrate how such an alliance could effectively challenge a resistant military was the "Tailhook scandal." In September 1991, the Las Vegas Hilton was chosen by the Tailhook Association for its annual convention of American fighter pilots who fly from aircraft carriers. These are the men actor Tom Cruise has made globally famous in his Hollywood film *Top Gun* and its recent sequel. "Tailhook" refers to the aircraft mechanism that catches a speeding fighter plane as it lands on the short, narrow deck of a seaborne aircraft carrier.

The Las Vegas Hilton Hotel was vibrating with masculine hubris. The US military had just returned home from its decisive victory against Saddam Hussein's Iraqi military in Kuwait. As they told it, the Navy's aircraft-carrier fighter pilots were major players in that victory.

The pilots weren't the only ones at the convention. The Tailhook Association had invited admirals and other senior Defense Department officials to attend, as well as private contractors who did business with the Pentagon. Less noticed were a handful of uniformed women, Navy officers who had come to Las Vegas to pressure the admirals to end their ban on women becoming aircraft-carrier fighter pilots.

Each all-male pilot squadron had organized its own "hospitality suite" in the Hilton, where its members partied and entertained guests. Over the years, the squadrons had become increasingly competitive, each trying to out-party the other. By 1991, some squadrons had hired women from Las Vegas nightclubs to perform in their suites as strippers. The male pilots had enhanced the party atmosphere of their suites by inviting young women students from the nearby colleges to join the fun.

In the spirit of militarized, manly fun, the pilots also had created a ritual for their hotel corridor. They called it "the gauntlet." Navy men lined either side of the corridor just outside the elevator and spun any woman visitor who emerged down the gauntlet.

The admirals and contractors meeting on the lower floors of the hotel didn't care. Just post-victory high jinks. All the pilots, after all, were officers; it was just "boys being boys."

Then the pilots made a mistake. A woman in civilian clothes exited the elevator, one woman among many. She was treated to the gauntlet's manhandling. Her name was Paula Coughlin. She was a navy officer, a lieutenant and a helicopter pilot. In 1991, she was assigned as an aide to an admiral. She reported to the admiral what had happened on the squadrons' party floor. He told her it was not important, to "move on." Paula Coughlin did not "move on." She became a whistleblower. She reported her experience to members of the House of Representatives' Armed Services Committee.

The media picked up the story. Sex, pilots, war, Las Vegas. Editors framed the story as a "scandal." Activists in the National Organization of Women (NOW), however, framed the Tailhook assaults as a violation of women's rights. Other women in the military framed it as added evidence of the sexism inside the military that had been damaging their careers for decades.

On the House Armed Services Committee at the time was Representative Pat Schroeder, a Democrat from Colorado. Schroeder was the first woman in the history of the US Congress to have a seat on the House Armed Services Committee. She was a feminist. She already had challenged the Pentagon on its policies toward military wives, and now she called congressional hearings. That made President George HW Bush and his Secretary of Defense, Dick Cheney, sit up and take notice.

Moreover, Schroeder, along with other women in the House, formed a public delegation to insist that heads roll. The Secretary of the Navy resigned. A new, more thorough investigation was launched. That investigation revealed not only the enabling assumption of senior Navy officers that male warriors need to "let off steam," but also a culture that informed the pilot squadrons' competitive misogynist "entertainments."[63]

The Tailhook scandal may have played a part in the Navy policymakers deciding, soon after, to lift the ban on women becoming fighter pilots. The first was Rosemary Mariner. She was one of the women officers who, in September 1991, had been downstairs at the Las Vegas Hilton lobbying admirals to permit women to become fighter pilots.

It is important not to overstate the 1991 feminist-informed alliance's achievements. Yes, the Navy was outed as institutionally misogynist. Yes, a secretary of the Navy was forced to resign. Yes, another barrier to women's full participation in the country's military was dismantled.

Yes, the women members of Congress, though few, showed that, if they allied with civilian feminists and with women in the military, they could compel a masculinized legislature to take proper action. Yes, many ordinary American civilians learned to be critical of their celebrated wartime heroes. Nonetheless, not one of the male Navy officers who sexually harassed and assaulted women in the Las Vegas hotel gauntlet was significantly punished. Prosecutors were stymied in part by the men's collective protection of each other. That is what the much-heralded "unit cohesion" can look like when it operates as a wall of silence to deprive women of their rights and dignity.

The American public, moreover, still continues to elevate the US military as one of their most trusted institutions. They flocked to see *Top Gun: Maverick*.

In 1991, Paula Coughlin was a young officer on her way up the Navy's career ladder. Three years later, Paula Coughlin resigned from the Navy. After winning court suits against both the Tailhook Association and the Las Vegas Hilton for negligence, she opened a yoga studio in Florida. This had not been her plan.

And "Tailhook" was not the end of American – nor Canadian, nor Australian, nor Irish – military men's sexual assaults on women in the military.[64] In fact, by the early 2000s, so many American women were leaving the military due to suffering from trauma caused by having been sexually assaulted by their male comrades that the US Department of Veterans' Affairs was compelled (under pressure from women veterans) to fund medical clinics to treat women veterans' post-assault trauma. The agency even introduced a new medical concept: Medical Sexual Trauma (MST).

∽

Nor should we minimize military men's violence against military women as somehow a "first world problem." Women's advocates who focus on the United Nations were inspired by the transnational #MeToo movement to investigate where in the sprawling United Nations organization men's sexual assaults on women were being perpetrated – and if and how they were being covered up.

An arena on which their feminist enquiries pulled back the curtain was international military peacekeeping operations. One of the first reports was conducted for an independent organization, the International Peace Institute. The authors were three feminist researchers with experience in investigating violence against women in war zones. Now they were investigating sexual violence inside precisely those organizations that were supposed to help end wartime violence: international blue-helmeted peacekeeping militaries.

Their report is *Blue on Blue*.[65]

The UN relies on member states to contribute police and military units to UN peacekeeping missions in conflict areas such as South Sudan, Somalia and the Central African Republic. The richer countries pay for UN peacekeeping, but are not contributing most of the peacekeepers. The countries contributing most of the peacekeeping troops are from the Global South: Bangladesh, South Korea, Nepal, Brazil, Fiji, India, Nigeria. These contributing member states' officials see the uniformed personnel they deploy as their own. On paper, both the contributing governments and the UN are responsible for ensuring that peacekeepers act according to codes of behavior, including prohibitions against abuse of women.

In practice, who takes the responsibility for tackling any uniformed personnel's misbehavior is always a bone of diplomatic contention. Women peacekeepers who suffer male colleagues' abuse while deployed on missions often fall into those diplomatic cracks.

It doesn't help that the ratio of men to women on UN peacekeeping missions is currently 9:1. One woman peacekeeper explained: "It's like you are in an oasis and there is a whole bunch of thirsty camels. I felt like a matador just deflecting the advances or the suggestive comments."[66]

Blue on Blue researchers found that women peacekeepers couldn't trust their superiors or UN officials to take serious action to investigate and hold accountable any abusive male soldiers, most of whom were higher ranking than the women they harassed or assaulted.

Another woman peacekeeper described what happened to one of her colleagues, when, as was common during peacekeepers' off-duty hours, a woman peacekeeper joined a male colleague for drinks: "This was a guy everyone thought was great because he gave great speeches on gender equality and on rights, and she used to write them for him and he abused her! She still hasn't gotten justice."[67]

∽

Where does this leave feminists? It has taken time for feminists in most countries to devote serious attention to those women who have joined militaries. Initially, it seemed too politically compromising. Yet, since the 1980s, the rapid increases in the numbers of women voluntarily enlisting – especially as so many governments have ended male conscription – have pushed feminist activists to take steps to support women in militaries.

Feminists in many countries, moreover, have concluded that military institutions are so influential in societal dynamics that their internal misogynist cultures cannot be allowed to go unchallenged.

This shift in feminist attention, however, has not persuaded women activists in most countries that women joining state military forces is the path toward liberation. The reliance of militaries on both secrecy and force continues to be at odds with the deeper values of feminist-informed democracy. At their cores, despite reforms, militaries remain patriarchal institutions and tools for patriarchal foreign policy.

FIVE

Women as Armed Insurgents Offer Feminist Caveats

THERE IS A SMALL museum in Ho Chi Minh City devoted to the Vietnamese women from the south who fought in the Viet Cong, first against the French and then the Americans. The stout, compact, five-foot-tall woman who met us at the entrance was dressed in her 1970s military uniform. Her chest of ribbons testified to her wartime valor.

This was 1993. The combined forces of the Viet Cong and North Vietnamese army had driven the last American soldiers out of then-Saigon almost two decades earlier. Vietnam was now an independent country, with its capital in Hanoi. But memories of women's roles in defeating the French and the Americans were being kept alive here in the women-initiated women's war museum. Fittingly, it was housed in a 1920s mansion once occupied by French colonial officials.

The retired officer proudly showed us the exhibits documenting the roles of women in the armed resistance movements. These women were fighters. They had taken up arms against the French colonial military, the US occupying military (and their South Korean, Australian and Filipino soldier allies) and the US-backed South Vietnam government's military, the "ARVN."

The museum's rooms were filled with photographs of armed women, as well as crafts that women insurgents had made while fighting. There were images of the iconic Trung Sisters, Trac and Nhi, still revered by the Vietnamese for having mounted elephants in CE 40 to lead the Vietnamese in their resistance against the first

Chinese occupation.[68] Paintings and sculptures of their twentieth-century descendants featured women fighters in combat positions, aiming their rifles skyward at American helicopters. Several of the most prominent exhibits showed images of an insurgent woman fighter holding a rifle in one arm while cradling an infant in the other. Insurgent women with rifles and infants. How many armed insurgent movements around the world have distributed a similar image? It is never clear who the image is designed to reassure. Perhaps the women fighters themselves, reassuring them that they are not sacrificing their feminine selves when they leave home to join a militarized insurgency. Or perhaps the image is intended by the insurgency's male leadership to win over local civilians who might otherwise fear that the insurgents mean not only to depose the colonial authorities and their local collaborators, but to also upset the society's conventional roles for women.[69]

Vietnamese women from the north also became armed fighters in these back-to-back wars, first as part of the nationalist Viet Minh insurgency fighting the French and then, in the 1960s, as members of the Hanoi-led North Vietnamese military fighting the Americans. These northern women also are celebrated with a museum, this one in Hanoi and more subject to the government's messaging. Here too, women combining anti-imperial fighting and motherhood is a curatorial theme. The most famous wartime achievement of these northern women, however, was carrying thousands of heavy ammunition boxes, down the mountainous Ho Chi Minh Trail, while under attack from American planes overhead.

Now, two generations later, northern Vietnamese women veterans, while officially celebrated on patriotic holidays, live precarious lives. Due to long-term injuries suffered when transporting ammunition, many women veterans could not marry after the war. Men did not want a woman who could not bear children. An injured, unmarried, childless woman was likely to be poor in post-war Vietnamese society.[70]

In the twenty-first century, the granddaughters of southern and northern women who fought in the anti-colonial insurgencies against the French and the Americans comprise the backbone of their country's export-dependent industries making garments and sneakers.

Independent labor union organizing among factory workers is strongly discouraged, not only by the brand-name apparel corporations such as Nike, North Face and H&M, but also by the export-reliant Hanoi government.

Today, women are almost invisible at upper levels of Vietnam's ruling party. In 2022, the Politburo was seventeen men and one woman. All four of the top party officials were men.[71]

What happened?

∽

It is a question posed by many women who made personal sacrifices to join anti-colonial and anti-dictatorial insurgent fighting forces.[72]

Women as fighters in anti-colonial and anti-autocratic insurgencies are legion. In Mexico, Spain, China, Algeria, Vietnam, Palestine, Guatemala, Nicaragua, El Salvador, Eritrea, Ethiopia, the Philippines, Sri Lanka, Kenya, Zimbabwe, Angola, Guinea-Bissau, Mozambique, Namibia, South Africa, Cuba, Northern Ireland, Nepal, Colombia and Myanmar, women have joined insurgent forces waging armed rebellion against oppressive states. They all have lessons to teach us about the dynamic entanglements of militarization, ideology, masculinization, patriarchy and women's genuine empowerment.

Generally, women do not voice regret about having joined those anti-colonial, anti-repression, anti-autocracy insurgent armed forces. They are proud. Rather, many of these veteran women fighters share a sense that their efforts have not produced the sort of post-liberation gender-equitable societies they had imagined they were struggling for. Out of their reflections about why that is so have come their caveats.

It's not as if there weren't earlier warnings. Algerian women's advocates warned their Palestinian sisters. Cuban women veterans shared their cautionary tales with the Nicaraguan women who joined the Sandinista movement. Zimbabwean fighting force veterans shared their cautions with South African ANC women.[73]

Today, Kurdish women fighting in the Turkish-Kurdish insurgency, Palestinian women active in their society's liberation movement, and

Myanmar women who have joined their society's multi-ethnic pro-democracy armed movement have listened. They have taken explicit steps so patriarchal history will not repeat itself. They do not want to be surprised when a seemingly inclusive, progressive fighting force produces a patriarchal post-insurgency state. Women in these current armed insurgent liberationist movements keep looking at their movement's own internal structures and asking, "Where are the women?" They seek recognition for traditionally "women's work" as serious political work. And they try to broaden the meanings of gender identity so they don't become calcified.[74]

∽

This chapter looks at the lessons offered by women who have served in what might be called progressive insurgent armed forces. Sometimes they are called revolutionaries, other times freedom fighters. They have chosen to take up arms against established repressive governments for liberationist causes.

There are other militarized insurgencies that are explicitly patriarchal – in particular, those armed movements that are religiously identified and motivated by fundamentalist ideologies. Some of them have included women, usually as wives, mothers and occasionally suicide bombers.[75] Those explicitly patriarchal armed groups are worth examining for their gendered dynamics and for the thoughts of the women who have allied themselves with those groups.

It is, though, the lessons crafted by women who have joined progressive, social justice-seeking armed groups – anti-colonial, anti-dictatorship, anti-racism armed groups – that feminists especially have had to weigh when thinking about war. It is women who take up arms for those liberationist causes that especially challenge all feminists to ask: when is militarized action compatible with – even, in furtherance of – feminist political goals?

Most progressive armed insurgent groups that have had as their goal removing colonial, neo-colonial and repressive autocratic regimes have recruited women. Many women, especially young women, have responded to those appeals. Their motivations have been diverse. Some of those women had already been active in their country's anti-colonial, socialist, pro-independence or pro-democracy unarmed movements. They decided to join the armed resistance only after the regime had escalated the coercive force to suppress those peaceful movements. This is true, for instance, of Nicaraguan, Kurdish and Myanmar women who have joined armed progressive groups.

Other women fighters have been new to the cause, but were galvanized by seeing their brothers, fathers or partners killed by government security forces. Still other women wanted to do more than be merely supportive caretakers of armed men. They wanted to fight. By taking up arms or contributing to the armed struggle in assorted ways, they believed, they could prove that they were equal to men in the resistance and should become equal beneficiaries of the fought-for liberation.[76]

Many of the men who became the leaders of armed anti-colonial, anti-dictatorship insurgencies have seen women joining their armed groups as a positive development and have actively recruited women. Nonetheless, over decades, it has become clear that most of these male leaders of liberation-seeking armed insurgencies, and the governing political parties that have grown out of those armed insurgent forces, have been less inclined to surrender masculinized privilege and power once they had achieved their insurgent objective of forming a new state.

Oddly, transforming an armed militarized insurgent group into a civilian political party often has intensified the group's patriarchal tendencies.

⌒

It was January in Helsinki. Fresh snow fell every night. As we walked along, the dry, pristine snow crunched pleasingly under our boots. Newly fallen snow might seem an odd backdrop for an intense discussion about Algerian women's myriad roles in the war that drove out the French colonizers. But, once we had taken off our ski caps and gloves, our Finnish feminist host, Eva Isaksson, made sure that that was exactly what we attended to.[77]

It was 1987. It had been twenty-five years since Algerian insurgents had overthrown the French colonial regime in 1962, twenty-five years during which Algerian anti-colonial insurgent women could assess their wartime contributions and what they had yielded. Marie-Aimée Hélie-Lucas led us in the accounting.

Marie-Aimée had joined the anti-colonial insurgency as a teenage girl and was twenty-four by the time the war had ended in an insurgent victory. She began by warning us (women from Germany, Denmark, US, UK, Switzerland, Chile, Ethiopia, Netherlands, Finland and France) not to swallow the misleading gender myths surrounding the Algerian insurgency. Contrary to the popular narratives, she explained, Algerian urban women – the sort featured in the globally viewed film *The Battle of Algiers* – were not the backbone of the anti-colonial insurgency. Likewise, Algerian women in combat roles, often held up internationally as models of the "liberated woman," were not the true heroes.

The gender realities of Algeria's insurgent anti-colonial warfare were quite different from the myths. Most of the tasks performed by women – at great risk of arrest and torture by the French – were performed by Algerian women living in the countryside. These were peasant women, lacking both literacy and paid work. Marie-Aimée Hélie-Lucas enumerated their insurgent tasks: "Guiding, hiding, feeding, carrying messages, buying arms, watching the French army moves and taking arms from those who had died." In addition, these rural women, she explained, sewed fighters' torn clothes, collected medicines, nursed the wounded, and raised money.

When we think of "fighters," she warned us, we need to vastly expand our notions of what "fighting" in an insurgency realistically entails. If we persist in picturing an insurgent fighter as someone wielding explosives or a gun, we will miss most of the women who contribute to any liberationist insurgency.

Even with such an expanded understanding of wartime tasks, however, Algerian women's contributions to the insurgency were marginalized by male observers and leaders limited by a patriarchal mindset. Marie-Aimée elaborated:

> ... if a man, at the risk of his life, carried food over long distances in the mountains, it is acknowledged that he was a fighter – while if a woman did so, she was only "helping" in her traditional and natural way of nurturing. If a man, at the risk of his life, hid armed fighters or "wanted" political leaders, he was certainly called a fighter – while if a woman did so, she was simply performing her normal woman's nurturing task.[78]

On that snowy Helsinki morning, Marie-Aimée Hélie-Lucas offered a feminist caveat: to fully account for women's contributions to any anti-colonial or anti-authoritarian insurgency, we need to do gender division of labor accounting and then go one step further: pay attention to the gendered meanings attached to playing each role. In any patriarchy, if what a woman does is defined as just acting according to her "natural" femininity, then that woman and her contribution can be minimized, trivialized, unrewarded and swept under history's rug.

Despite the unfairness of the divisions of labor and the meanings assigned to feminized roles, insurgent girls and women did not protest – until it was too late. Looking back, Marie-Aimée reflected that she and her fellow Algerian women insurgents internalized three mutually reinforcing gendered beliefs handed down by the male leaders: first, the solidarity that was necessary to defeat the French required unbroken discipline; second, protesting any intra-movement gender unfairness only bolstered the colonial oppressors and thus was a betrayal of the liberationist cause; third, women who willingly fulfilled their feminized assigned wartime gendered roles were laying the foundation for a post-colonial nation that would be authentically Algerian.

These wartime dictates and the beliefs legitimizing them formed the basis for the new, post-insurgency Algerian state. Two decades later, in 1984, the revolutionary party was still in control of the state. Its leaders passed what many Algerian women veteran insurgents deemed the final straw: a new Family Code that denied women's right to marry (women could only be given by men in marriage), denied women the right to divorce and restricted women's inheritance rights. Women veterans responded by doing what they had not done during the war or in the first years following liberation: they organized public protests. But to no avail. The Family Code became law.

During the 1980s, as during wartime, Algeria's male leaders admonished women veterans, their former insurgent comrades, that "now" was not the time to publicly criticize the party in power, that even twenty years after overthrowing French rule, the party-controlled state was too fragile, faced too many external enemies to allow such a women's protest. Marie-Aimée Hélie-Lucas summarized the liberationist male elite's view: "Defending women's rights 'now' – this now being *any* historical moment – is always a betrayal of the people, of the revolution, of Islam, of national identity, of cultural roots . . ."[79]

∽

The Nicaraguan women who joined in the 1970s Sandinista armed resistance against the oppressive Somoza regime knew of the inspiring narratives of the Algerian and, especially, the Cuban revolutions: women could be fighters; women could be men's equals; women could play important roles in creating a truly liberated society.

Fresh from their victory over Somoza's repressive regime, Sandinista women were eager to respond to the questions put to them by Margaret Randall in 1979. They trusted Randall because they knew her to be a supporter of women who had fought in the 1950s Cuban revolution.[80]

Margaret Randall interviewed a young woman insurgent named Julia. She was twenty-six years old and pregnant with her fifth child. She wanted Randall to know how she had become involved in the Sandinista insurgency. Her story intertwined impoverished girlhood, childcare, low-paid work, illiteracy and fear:

My mom died when I was thirteen. She had sixteen children: eight boys and eight girls. After my mom died my father married another woman and abandoned us completely. So I had to go out to work right away. I worked cleaning a factory and earned 50 *cordobas* a month. I'll tell you, I never set foot in a school because I had to work . . . I only began to read and write after I got involved in the struggle . . .

Before the victory you couldn't say publicly, "I belong to the Sandinista National Liberation Front." People were scared. But I got involved . . . My first activity was occupying a church for a hunger strike. I wanted to find out, for myself, what it was like to be involved. I told myself maybe I'd learn something and get rid of my fears.[81]

Nicaraguan women who joined the Sandinistas during the 1970s told of learning how to read and write, becoming confident, realizing that politics was not something only men did. In the process, Sandinista women learned how to hide insurgents. They developed skills in raising the consciousnesses of other women, especially poor women. They discovered that even doing domestic chores could contribute to the larger struggle against oppression. Over time, they told Margaret Randall, they also learned that women had to organize as women within the insurgency, both to empower women and to persuade insurgent men to take seriously women and their domestic work.

Margaret Randall stayed attentive. She wanted to know how women insurgents would fare after the Sandinistas controlled the state, turned themselves into an electorally competitive political party, then lost a national election and became a civilian opposition party. She returned to Nicaragua in 1991 to interview the women she had first met in 1979.

Women veterans told her they had become aware that the top-down power system that was necessary for waging an armed struggle was not appropriate for a political party meant to win popular elections and effectively govern in peacetime. Michele Najlis explained:

Of course, we had to have a vertical line of command to topple the dictator – and afterward to fight against the counter-revolution [the "Contra" counter-insurgency funded by the US government], at least in the war zones. But that top-down discipline in Managua [Nicaragua's capital], in our political life, what was the justification for that? And you know, a great many of us questioned it, but we had no possibility of being heard. Not really . . .[82]

As part of that continued post-war militarized command structure, the women's organization that women had created inside the Sandinista movement during the war was losing its autonomy, becoming merely an arm of the centralized political party. Men at the top didn't seem to care about women's own realities and political needs. Michele Najlis continued:

> I remember the day Daniel [Ortega, one of the senior leaders of the Sandinista armed movement and of the post-war party] said something about abortion being "one of those exotic ideas imported from Europe and the United States" . . . Doctors at the Berta Calderon Hospital told him, "Comandante, two hundred and fifty women a year die of botched abortions in this hospital alone. And that's not counting those who never make it to the hospital." But he kept insisting it was "intellectual claptrap." The same for family planning. He didn't want to hear about it . . . All Daniel could say was that we needed to reproduce because the war was killing so many of our combatants!

From the 1980s into the '90s, the political dilemma became increasingly acute for many of the Sandinista women who had made such sacrifices during the war against the Somoza regime. At such a precarious time for the country, how could women's advocates stay true to the values of the revolution when the political party that claimed to represent those values seemed to be betraying them both in its internal modes of operation and in its public policy priorities? For some of these Sandinista women veterans, the path out of this dilemma was to organize women autonomously from the party. In taking this step, they hoped to free themselves from masculinized top-down control and to develop priorities that more closely matched diverse Nicaraguan women's genuine needs.

∽

No two anti-repression insurgencies are identical. The Chinese revolution was not a mere template for the Vietnamese revolution. The Cuban revolution was not simply replicated by the Nicaraguans. Today, Myanmar's pro-democracy insurgency is not a mere copycat version of the Nepalese insurgency. Each armed insurgency is shaped by the strength or decay of the repressive state it is challenging and by the ethnic and regional rivalries or alliances that are at work in the society. Each armed insurgency is shaped by the width of the gap between rural and urban people and by the levels of interference (oppositional or supportive) from neighboring and distant states. Each armed insurgency is shaped by the coherence or fragmentation of the political movement out of which the armed rebellion has grown.

All the influential factors are hard to keep in mind when one is trying to compare any two anti-repression insurgencies. Still, that list is not complete. Insurgencies also differ in their internal and external gender politics. They differ from one another in what proportion of their active supporters (all kinds of "fighters") are women and whether those women are able to reach senior posts in the armed insurgency. Insurgencies, moreover, differ from one another in how explicit or vague their usually male leaders are in their wartime commitments to gender equity as integral to the sought-after liberation. Each leader of an armed insurgency also shows different levels of tolerance – or intolerance – toward its women participants' efforts to develop their own organizations within the struggle, and how much genuine autonomy they "allow" those women's groups to cultivate.

Crucially, insurgencies differ in how much experience their women participants already have gained in recognizing the workings of patriarchy. Each insurgency is distinctive in what, if any, cautionary lessons their women participants have garnered from insurgent women veterans from other countries.

A peaceful, if militant, civil-society protest movement, of course, is not immune from patriarchy. But when an anti-repression movement turns into an armed movement – often in response to intolerable state brutality – the risks of patriarchal privileging of certain sorts of masculinity and the marginalization of anything deemed "feminine" will intensify. As many women who have made extraordinary sacrifices to support armed liberationist insurgencies have testified, when a civil movement becomes an armed insurgency, it is likely to simultaneously become top-down in its structure, intolerant of internal dissent and masculinized in its culture, celebrating the combat fighter. This is what militarization fosters.

∽

Myanmar's current nation-wide armed insurgent movement was created in response to the military's coup d'etat in February 2021. In the five years preceding the coup, Myanmar women's advocates had experienced a time of civil-society activism more open than any in Myanmar's past two generations. This made the timing of Myanmar's insurgency quite unlike those in Vietnam, Algeria, Nicaragua or many of the other armed rebellions that had begun after years of intensifying state repression and brutality. By early 2021, there were openly feminist ideas being expressed in Myanmar's popular and academic spaces, and women's activist groups were organizing to raise public awareness and pressure the Myanmar government to address gender inequities.

For decades, Myanmar had been under military rule. Opposition parties were banned, elections jettisoned, pro-democracy leaders detained. During the early 2000s, there was mounting international pressure on the ruling generals to allow at least a partial democratization. During this brief era of relative opening, however, Myanmar was far from genuinely democratic. The agreement in 2015 with the military that saw Nobel Peace laureate Aung San Suu Kyi freed from her fifteen-year detention also allowed the electoral political party she led to share state power with the long-ruling military. It did not end the generals' dominant role in the country's politics. Furthermore, the multi-front war that the ethnically Burman-dominated state military had been waging for decades against autonomy-seeking ethnic groups in its border regions – the Shan, Kachin, Karen and Mon – persisted. Finally, it was during this period of relative openness that the military – with the apparent support of Aung San Suu Kyi – mounted a brutal attack on another ethnic minority, the Rohingya.[83]

To protest the military's February 2021 takeover, led by General Min Aung Hlaing, (which included the jailing of Aung San Suu Kyi and other civilian leaders of her political party), thousands of Myanmar civilian women and men took to the streets in cities and towns around the country. Aung San Suu Kyi, while roundly condemned abroad for her refusal to stand up to the military that was brutally displacing the besieged Rohingya minority, remained for many local people the symbol of democracy. Civil servants refused to go to work. Doctors and nurses went on strike. Students boycotted classes. Myanmar's feminists were deeply engaged in the anti-coup protests. As ordinary life came to a standstill, the military responded to peaceful protests with escalating violence. For weeks, despite mounting injuries, deaths and mass arrests, the protestors maintained their determined peaceful protests.

Women came out to protest in droves. They represented teachers, garment workers and medical workers, all sectors of the twenty-first-century Myanmar economy dominated by women. They not only led marches, they attended to the civilian wounded. They told reporters that they saw the military's coup as an attempt to roll back democratization, and, simultaneously, to reimpose a patriarchal order, an order that, in the generals' minds, was justified because women were deemed to be weak and impure. As Ma Ei Thinzar, a twenty-seven-year-old woman activist and former political prisoner, explained: "Women took the frontier position in the fight against dictatorship because they believed it is our cause."[84]

Militarized violence, including rape, had been wielded for decades by the Tatmadaw (as the military has called itself) against the women of Myanmar's defiant minority groups. After the 2021 coup, the country's ethnic Burman majority, mostly town and city dwellers, experienced that violence first-hand.

Seeking to explain the seemingly limitless violence that Myanmar's soldiers unleashed on their fellow citizens, long-time *New York Times* journalist Hannah Beech described how a highly masculinized and ethnicized insular institutional culture had been carefully constructed by the Tatmadaw generals over the eighty years since the country won its independence from Britain:

> What we have discovered is that this is a deeply insular, secretive culture that is unlike any other military in the world . . . From the beginning, when they are in boot camp, the troops are taught one lesson above all, which is that they are the guardians of the country and the religion – Buddhism – that will crumble without them . . .

That is, the 2021 coup was not the start of the story. Nor was the military's deliberate recruitment of young men from the country's dominant ethnic and religious community itself enough to explain soldiers firing so willingly on civilians, who, in Yangon and other cities, shared their ethnicity and religion. Hannah Beech continued:

> . . . Soldiers live apart from the rest of society. They work apart from the rest of society. And they have an entire ecosystem that's dedicated just to them . . . The Tatmadaw has its own banks, hospitals, schools, universities, insurance agencies, mobile network operators, stock options and even vegetable farms . . . They don't see the protesters as humans, as fellow Burmese . . . Anybody who questions the military is fraying the unity of the country.[85]

By the end of March 2021, the extreme violence used against peaceful protestors and the growing sense that the military was unmovable, plus protestors' shared conviction that the open civil society that they had created over the past five years was worth risking their lives to sustain, convinced many of Myanmar's pro-democracy civilians that they had no choice but to leave the towns, escape to the jungle and once there to build an armed resistance.

Women as well as men joined the pro-democracy armed resistance. Among them were women who had been politically conscious activists before the coup. As one young woman who had fled to the jungle told a reporter: "I decided to risk my life and fight back any possible way I can . . . If we oppose nationwide in unison, we will make the military have sleepless nights and insecure lives, just as they have done to us."[86]

"Nationwide in unison." This was not a given. It was a goal. For many of the women protestors-turned-armed-insurgents, it was the first time they had had to think seriously about their relationships to women in the Shan, Kachin, Mon, Karen and Rohingya ethnic communities. They would need to build trust with those women to become allies in their common war against the government's military. After decades of not being directly engaged in solidarity with the ethnic minority women, building this trust would not be easy. The newly armed city women would have to learn to treat minority ethnic group women with respect, would need to see them as their tutors. They would have to learn from these minority women how to move in a land-mined terrain, how to obtain food, how to survive constant aerial attacks and ground assaults. They would need to absorb the lessons these women could teach them about how to survive militarized rape.[87]

At the same time, politically conscious women who joined Myanmar's new pro-democracy armed resistance would need to be on the alert for the militarization of the movement, a militarization that could breed top-down hierarchy and privilege particular forms of masculinity – a masculinization that has so often accompanied the transition of a civilian movement to an armed insurgency.

∽

When the armed insurgency ends – either in an ouster of the repressive regime or in a negotiated settlement that provides the armed movement with significant post-war political influence – women insurgents are on high alert: will the armed insurgency produce a post-war civilian political party that perpetuates the hierarchical, silencing, masculinized tendencies of the armed movement?

One of the hardest gender lessons that has been crafted by women insurgents over the past seventy years is this: do not rely on the promise that achieving some other goal – ending colonial rule, ending racialized supremacy, ousting an autocrat, gaining the movement's political ascendancy, achieving national independence – will "automatically" bring with it the end of masculinized privilege, patriarchy.

We are all learning that achieving and sustaining women's rights and, with them, gender equity, takes specific commitments to ending masculinized privilege and profoundly changing our understandings of gendered authority and justice. Moreover, achieving gender equity requires deliberate actions to be taken by those at the top – during the revolution and in the aftermath of the revolution.

Being in genuine feminist solidarity with those women who are taking the risk to participate in a justice-seeking armed insurgency, likewise, calls for us who are outsiders to be energetically attentive to the gender dynamics within the insurgent movement. That, in turn, means we need to resist shrinking our admiration down to the weapons-carrying insurgent women.

Most importantly, insurgent women have taught us, we need to develop a long attention span. We should not rely on the achievement of a so-called "larger" goal to automatically bring women's liberation.

"Automatically," it turns out, is never automatic.

SIX

Wounds Matter –
Wounds Are Gendered

"Casualties." it's such an unhelpful term. Experts and statisticians use "casualties" to cover both war dead and war wounded. The dead and the wounded, however, carry different meanings and send out significantly different ripples of gendered consequences.

If pushed, wartime counters will fall back on counting just the dead:

- Battle of the Somme: 300,000
- Pearl Harbor attack: 2,403
- Atomic bombings of Hiroshima and Nagasaki, low estimate: 110,000
- Korean war: 5,000,000
- Srebrenica massacre, low estimate: 8,372
- Rwandan genocide, low estimate: 500,000

Historians admit that counting even only the war dead is imprecise.[88] It is also sometimes flawed with deliberate omissions by the official war-dead counters.[89] But counting all the "casualties," both the war dead and the war wounded, seems to border on the impossible.

Not explicitly counting the war wounded – civilian and military – leaves us with a dangerously incomplete accounting of the true costs of any war.[90]

Many of the wounded – women, men, girls, boys – survive the wars. They are destined to live with their wounds into the post-war years. Their disfigured faces, their blindness, their impaired hearing, their awkward limps, their absent arms, their shattered legs, their reproductive incapacities, their nightmares – each will shape not only their own lives, but the lives of those who care for them.

Furthermore, failing to pay close and ongoing attention to any war's wounded underestimates the roles women play as low-paid care workers and unpaid caregiving mothers and wives in any war or post-war. It is a failure that carries significant political risk.

Our inattention to wounds, the wounded and their caregivers plays into the hands of the militarizers, those who hope that we will support the current war or accept the next war, and thus want us to imagine wars are not so costly.

If we reject such militarized shrugs and, instead, practice a feminist attentiveness to wounds and the wounded, we will become more curious about the lives and thoughts of the women who serve as nurses, domestic workers, wives and mothers in the wake of armed conflicts. We will pay attention to both Tamil and Sinhalese women's lives following their country's decades-long Sri Lankan war; to ethnically diverse Myanmar women in their country's ongoing, multi-front war; to Black, Latino, Indigenous and white women's lives in the wake of the long US wars in Iraq and Afghanistan; to both Baganda and Acholi Ugandan women in post-war Uganda; to the communally diverse Northern Irish, Rwandan and Bosnian women in the aftermaths of their precariously ended wars; to Palestinian, Afghan, Kashmiri, Sudanese, Syrian and Congolese women in the seemingly unending wars in Palestine, Afghanistan, Kashmir, Sudan, Syria and Congo.

When asked why she featured women's perspectives in her fictional accounts of the Trojan wars, novelist Pat Barker explained: "It's women who carry the can long-term; not exclusively – some men become carers for their wounded sons – but mostly it's women, long after the politicians have forgotten."[91]

Our taking seriously the complex experiences, labors, emotions and ideas of those women serving as the caregivers for the war wounded will make us all more realistic about the full and long-lasting consequences of war. If we practice attentive curiosity about these women's complex wartime and post-war lives, we may slow down, even reverse, the march of militarization.

⌒

War-waging governments depend on us to *not* count the wounded. They rely on us to act as though war wounds and the war wounded don't really matter.

There are plenty of incentives for us to not count or to lose track of the women and men, girls and boys who suffer wounds in war: "Well, at least they survived." Or: "Someone is probably looking after them." Or: "It's too ghastly to look at them."

Governments do their part in helping us to be inattentive to war wounds and war wounded. That is the point of the militarized concept "collateral damage." It naturalizes wounds: "Well, that's just what happens in war." *Anything that can be naturalized can be made to not matter.* If wounds and the wounded can be naturalized by sweeping them into the dismissive concept of "collateral damage," they won't matter. If they don't matter, we won't worry. If they don't matter, we won't bother to find out who is responsible.

Officials and commanders have several reasons for wanting to minimize tallies of both wounds and the wounded. First, wounded civilians and wounded soldiers make clear the pain that comes with war. War is not just about identity, courage and solidarity. Pain is woven into war. Secondly, wounded soldiers are the responsibility of the government or the commanders of any fighting force. With that responsibility comes expenditures of scarce resources, whether financial or medical. Consequently, military strategists have incentives to deny, underestimate or hide the wounded.

To sustain our collective inattention to wounds and the wounded, war strategists do their best to keep us from seeing the wounds and the wounded. That is why British historian Ana Carden-Coyne's decision to mount a centenary exhibition of World War I war artists' work was so daring. Even one hundred years after that brutal global conflict, it was hard to stand there in the Manchester Art Gallery in 2017 and look unblinkingly at the paintings she selected: artists' unflinching portrayals of wounded soldiers.[92] Art works hidden from the public during World War I were finally here on display. If one did not divert one's gaze, one would have to come face to face with the blood, the gash, the grimace, the agony.

These are not the sorts of art works that boost wartime home front morale. Better, militarizers strategize, to keep these canvases in storage until some later date, when (if) the sensitive public is ready to face war's cruel realities.

∽

Wartime officials and military strategists are made uncomfortable by women as male soldiers' widows (they haven't yet had to deal with many men who have lost their wives or husbands as soldiers killed in war). A woman widowed by war can carry moral weight. That makes widows politically dangerous. The public might be less willing to support the next war if the last war's widows were known to be poorly treated. War widows – especially those women from the country's dominant racial/ethnic group whose husbands were serving as the state's soldiers when they were killed – need to be ceremonially recognized and paid modest pensions. They need to be celebrated for their patriotic sacrifice. If handled correctly, that can sustain a society's militarization. The feminization of sacrifice, after all, is integral to patriarchal war waging.

Women as unpaid caregivers of both wounded soldiers and wounded civilians, however, pose a trickier political problem for the proponents of militarization. War-waging governments and militarized rebel commanders hope that the wounded can be kept out of view. Placing them in private homes is thus safer than letting them linger in crowded hospital wards. But home care requires the mobilization of women. It is thus women who are called upon to provide private, domestic, unpaid home care to the war wounded – civilians as well as fighters. They need to provide that care not just during the war but for years after the war. And they need to provide it without complaining.

Privately caring for war-wounded civilians and soldiers is demanding work. One has to lift the wounded into and out of the bathtub. One has to cook the wounded's favorite, digestible foods and help them eat. One has to boost the wounded's sagging morale, yet stay realistic oneself. One has to not panic when nightmares erupt in the middle of the night. One has to hone diplomatic skills to keep the wounded connected to relatives and friends. One has to learn how to plough the fields and fix the blown-out fuse and stalled car. If one is caring for a war-wounded child one has to remember this is just a child, and stay patient. If one is caring for a war-wounded adult, one has to avoid treating him or her as a child. Paperwork. One has to develop the stamina to handle stacks of bureaucratic paperwork.[93]

Women as wives and as mothers in many societies offer unpaid demanding care because they are personally devoted to the girls or boys, or adult women or men, who have been wounded by war's rifle shots, land mines, shrapnel, artillery fire or aerial bombs. Women offer that care, too, because they have come to believe that providing that care – for weeks, for years – is integral to their own sense of themselves as a good mother or a loyal wife. They also may offer that care to the war-wounded members of their extended families, despite the toll it takes on their own health and financial security, because their relatives and neighbors expect it of them. In most societies it is risky for any woman to be seen as a "bad mother" or an "uncaring, selfish wife."

If widely held militaristic ideas frame unpaid, uncomplaining caring for the war wounded as patriotic, then the stakes for the wounded's mother or wife become even greater.

Be honest with yourself: what would be your own reaction to hearing that a woman had divorced her veteran amputee husband?

∽

Feminists have learned never to dismiss or trivialize care – what care entails, who provides it and at what cost, who pays for it, who benefits. They have learned to keep in mind the interactions of gender, class and race while taking seriously caring and caregivers – the unpaid and the low-paid. Caretakers' motivations and migrations, their hardships and strategies have been treated by feminists as important topics of investigation and policy analysis. By taking seriously the diverse lives of mothers, wives, nurses, domestic workers, childcare and eldercare workers, feminists have turned a bright light on intimate politics, state politics and international politics – and the connections between them.[94]

Paying deliberate attention to both unpaid and low-paid caregivers has prepared feminists to keep their eyes wide open when assessing the politics of the war wounded.

In their own analyses of any given war, journalists and policy analysts rarely interview the researchers and activists who have investigated what feminists now call "the care economy." They should. If they did, they might draw up a more reliable accounting of a war's true long-term implications.

The war wounded and their caretakers exist in history. That is, neither are static. Nor are they identical over time from country to country or from class to class. Rich war-waging countries, for instance, have developed sophisticated medivac systems to get their wounded soldiers quickly off the battlefield and into fully equipped hospitals. "MASH" units – now mainly imagined as they are portrayed in re-runs of the popular television sitcom series, *M*A*S*H* – were, in the 1950s, a major innovation for providing military medical care to American wounded close to the front during the Korean War. The care given to wounded soldiers by the doctors, nurses and medics in a MASH unit was a major improvement over the care that Vera Brittain and her wartime nursing colleagues could provide to British wounded soldiers near the battlefronts in World War I, while that, in turn, was a far cry from the crude medical care received by war wounded during the 1860s US Civil War.

By contrast, Sudanese, Somali and Congolese wounded soldiers today are not the ones who are being taken quickly from their battlefields by helicopters to awaiting well-equipped hospitals. It does matter if you are a wounded soldier fighting for a poor government or for an affluent government.

The medical care that wounded soldiers from most countries currently receive, though, comes first from military medics, then from nurses and doctors, and, later, if they are lucky, from physical and occupational therapists. The dynamic among these wartime medical workers is deeply gendered and hierarchical. Across otherwise dissimilar countries, most of the wounded soldiers are men, as are most of the military medics, while most of the military nurses are women, most of the doctors are men, and a majority of the OT and PT professionals are women.

Wartime nursing and nurses are routinely overlooked by military experts: nurses are assumed by so-called experts to be "merely" women performing feminized care work. Feminist historians, though, assume nothing. They have taken seriously the racialized, globalized histories of peacetime and wartime nursing.

Not for them, therefore, the trivializing myth of Florence Nightingale as the proper Victorian lady in a long dress with her lantern faintly lighting the way through the crowded wartime hospitals of the Crimea. Instead, feminist historians and museum curators have uncovered Florence Nightingale the recruiter and trainer of secular nurses, the critic of lax medical protocols and the reformer of inefficient hospital administration. This is the same Nightingale whom they document chastising negligent male military surgeons, prioritizing wounded rank and file soldiers over wounded officers, lobbying the Minister of War for more supplies, and adeptly influencing male newspaper war correspondents who were shocked by the appalling conditions under which British soldiers were fighting, dying and enduring injuries during the government's Crimean War.[95]

Moreover, this was the Florence Nightingale, feminist researchers show, who was not afraid of feminized hospital labor. Integral to her nursing of wounded men in the Crimean War were cleaning kitchens and wards, preparing nutritious foods, dressing soldier-patients in clean shirts and making their beds with freshly laundered linens. While her British male surgeon colleagues disdained such womanly labors, Nightingale, who had studied the emerging science of germs in European clinics, saw cooking, cleaning, doing laundry and making beds as essential to the successful recovery of wounded soldiers.[96]

With advancements in battlefield medicine since Nightingale's time have come higher rates of survival among wounded soldiers. That's the good news. Those higher survival rates translate into more and more mothers and wives being needed to privately, uncomplainingly care for those surviving wounded soldiers when they return home. That is more problematic.

∽

Who counts as "war wounded"? Is a soldier suffering from PTSD officially counted among the wartime "wounded"? Is a woman soldier diagnosed with military sexual trauma counted as "wounded"? Does a soldier wounded by the "friendly fire" of his own comrades deserve to be listed among the war wounded? What about a woman civilian or a male soldier who was living or stationed downwind from an above-ground nuclear bomb test who later suffers a miscarriage or develops cancer: is she or he tallied among the "war wounded"? And how should officials categorize sick American, Korean, Australian or Filipino soldiers who served in Vietnam when the US sprayed the toxic defoliant, Agent Orange? Or an Afghan or US soldier who was stationed near a toxic military "burn pit": which of them should be listed among the war wounded?

Governments routinely try to shrink the official categories of war wounded for several reasons. Narrowing the criteria for being officially included among the war wounded goes hand in hand with labeling many wounded as merely "collateral damage" and privatizing feminized care of the war wounded. Together, these three political maneuvers – narrowing the criteria for what officially counts as war wounds, wielding the concept of "collateral damage," and feminizing the unpaid labor of caring for the war wounded – lower the financial and political costs of waging a war. They make war-wagers less responsible and war more palatable.

∽

The chair stands two stories tall. It looms over the entrance to what originally was the League of Nations and now is the headquarters of the United Nations in Geneva.

The giant chair is a straight-backed four-legged chair, the sort one might find in any modest home. Three of its long legs reach to the ground. The fourth leg is jaggedly broken.

This is a monument to a wartime wound.

The jagged leg of the four-legged towering chair represents the leg shattered by the unsuspecting person or animal who steps on a land mine – during a war or a generation after a war.

Land mines are cheap to make, buy and deploy. They are much more expensive to find, deactivate and remove. When laid under the ground, they are invisible. Their deadly explosives last for years. Most morally damning, land mines are *indiscriminate*: they are not designed to target a soldier or a tank. They will explode and rip into the lower body of a farmer, a cow, a child or a person walking to market.

Before the Russian military launched its invasion of Ukraine, organizations monitoring land mines estimated that there were 110,000,000 land mines buried in at least sixty countries around the world. Some may have been buried during World War II.

It was pictures of wounded children with amputated legs and arms shattered by land mines that helped build an international civil-society movement in the 1990s that called for the banning of land mines. Women were among the campaign's global activists, including Jody Williams, co-founder of the International Campaign to Ban Land mines and, later, Nobel Peace Prize laureate. The campaign's success took the form of the 1997 Mine Ban Treaty. As of 2022, 164 of the world's governments had ratified the Mine Ban Treaty. Among those governments that have refused to ratify the treaty are Russia, the US, China, Egypt, Israel, North Korea, South Korea, Pakistan, India and Saudi Arabia.[97]

Demining has become a significant job category in post-war countries such as Cambodia, Bosnia and Angola. It takes weeks of technical training to qualify as a deminer. Still, it is a dangerous occupation. Deminers live with constant uncertainty. Nonetheless, belonging to a local demining team brings a salary and the social status of being a community-valued, technically skilled person. Demining consequently has been thought of as a man's job. Demining teams have been masculinized teams. Slowly, however, gender equity has been coming to demining. The UN and local groups have joined together to encourage rural women to train to become deminers.[98]

In wartime Ukraine, women trying to supplement their meager wartime diets walked into their local forests to hunt for mushrooms. They were aware that they risked stepping on land mines buried there by retreating Russian troops. According to Ukraine's emergency service providers, victims of land mine explosions have come from all nine of the country's provinces. Ukrainian officials pleaded with citizens not to go mushroom hunting. But, for many Ukrainian civilians, walking into the forest to hunt mushrooms was not only a dietary necessity; it was an act of defiance: mushroom hunting was what peace should feel like.[99]

During the same war, Ukrainian male soldiers who have had their legs amputated due to land mine wounds have become symbols of national wartime resilience. A portion of these men has been sent to the United States to be fitted with the most up-to-date prosthetics.[100]

Since 2000, American defense officials have invested in developing advanced prosthetics and the physical therapy regimens required for amputees to effectively use them. It helped the war-waging government to showcase wounded male soldiers' resilience. That, in turn, made the wars in Iraq and Afghanistan appear less costly in human suffering, at least to civilians on the American home front. The wounded male soldier being able to recover to the point that he could, with his high-tech prosthetic, live an active, masculine life after a devastating injury became a political priority during their waging of the long wars in Iraq and Afghanistan. Those wars both featured enemy forces' use of ground explosives. Amputees came to represent the wars' tolls.

If American male veteran amputees could be shown on the Pentagon website playing ice hockey, if they could appear on television competing in the Paralympics, maybe voters at home wouldn't withdraw their support for the war. Maybe teenage boys would still talk to the army recruiter when he visited their high school.

While it is rebuilding wounded male soldiers' sense of masculine mobility, strength and self-esteem that is the officials' chief goal, medical personnel working with the amputees have learned that their mission will succeed only if they and the soldier-amputee have the physical and emotional support of the wounded male soldier's wife or mother, or both.[101]

Ruslan Tyshchenko, a forty-four-year-old Ukrainian male engineer, had volunteered to lay mines in an eastern region of Ukraine in order to slow down the advance of Russian tanks (despite Ukraine being a signatory to the Mine Ban Treaty). A Russian tank fired at him, exploding the mine he had strapped to his left leg. Gravely wounded, but still alive, Tyshchenko was rescued by his comrades. He later joined the small number of severely wounded Ukrainian male soldiers flown to an American clinic in Maryland to be fitted with an advanced model of a prosthetic leg and to receive the intensive therapy required to live with it.

The American veterans' charity that helped fund the prosthetics treatment also paid for Ruslan Tyshchenko's wife, Iryna, to fly from Ukraine to Maryland. Her mission: to support her husband during his painful recovery. To ward off the expected depression that so many amputee soldiers experience, Iryna told a journalist, she would reassure her husband that he was still accepted and loved. She promised him that when they got home to Ukraine, Ruslan would remain the head of the family. For instance, she promised her husband he would still be the one counted on to make the morning coffee.[102]

∽

The giant chair stands on its three remaining legs. Standing there looking up at it, one has to imagine the invisible woman keeping it balanced upright, trying to repair the fourth jagged leg, whispering, "You are still my favorite chair."

SEVEN

Make Wartime Rape Visible

"LOOTPILLAGEANDRAPE."

Stealing a chicken, laying waste to crops, sexually assaulting a local woman. For generations, all three abusive actions seemed equivalent. All three seemed inevitable. All three were trivialized. A male soldier robs a farmer of her poultry and burns down her family's fields of ripening wheat; of course, he'll then rape the farmer's teenage daughter.

Feminist researchers, lawyers and forensic investigators, together with local women's healthcare and anti-violence advocates, have challenged this lazy narrative. They have rejected both the trivialization of wartime rape and the naturalization of men's sexual assaults. They have argued, instead, that wartime sexual abuse of women has its own distinctive politics. They have asserted that it is crucial that we make men's wartime sexual abuse of women explicitly visible and subject it to careful investigation.

To do that, we need to be systematically curious. We need to investigate individual male rapists' assaults on women (and on some men) – in Bucha, in Kigali, in the Kachin region of Myanmar – while also asking whether there have been patterns to those seemingly random acts. Only by simultaneously investigating individual acts of sexual abuse and mapping possible patterns of those acts will we be able to hold accountable the wartime rapists, as well as those people who enable and protect those male rapists.

The feminist lesson: by becoming respectfully, patiently curious about women's experiences of sexual violence in war, and naming and holding accountable the rapists and their enablers, women's rights during and after wars can be effectively secured.[103]

∽

Feminist researcher Dyan Mazurana and her colleagues, together with researchers from Amnesty International, focused their curiosity in 2021 on how women in Ethiopia were experiencing the escalating armed conflict in their country. These investigators were not satisfied with the dominant narrative of ethnic rivalry between the Tigray and the central government, as if ethnicity explained everything.

Ethnicity, as well as race and religious communalism, may explain a lot about the causes and pathways of any violent social conflict, but they never explain everything, not in Ethiopia, Bosnia, Guatemala, the US, India, Myanmar, Iraq or Syria. Patriarchy in its extreme form – misogyny – always must be weighed and, where found, explicitly charted.

In Ethiopia's armed conflict, researchers documented scores of military men's sexual assaults on Ethiopian women in what appeared to be a pattern. It was a pattern of abuse clear enough for these feminist investigators to conclude that men's wartime rapes of women were being wielded systematically as a "weapon of war."

Mazurana and her colleagues identified the wartime rapists as male soldiers in both the Eritrean and Ethiopian state militaries. Both militaries were deployed by their autocratic governments to put down a rebellion by ethnic Tigrays. Mazurana's research team discovered that the male soldiers of both governments waged that war by systematically – that is, consciously, deliberately, purposefully – perpetrating rapes on ethnic Tigray women, as well as on some ethnic Tigray men. What they uncovered reminded them of the patterns of men's ethnically motivated sexual assaults they had seen documented in the Bosnia and Rwanda wars thirty earlier. There, feminist journalists, activists and healthcare workers learned to take women's experiences of armed conflict seriously. Similarly, according to Mazurana's 2021 report for the World Peace Foundation:

Testimony provides evidence of rape occurring in [Tigray] victims' homes in front of their families. They were dragged out and raped in public. They were raped as they sought out food and water. School girls were raped on their way to classes.

Nor did Mazurana and her co-researchers find these rapes to be haphazard, merely the actions of random male soldiers acting individually under the cover of the "fog of war":

There is a degree of organization, forethought and intent needed to set up rape camps [in former hospitals], line up rapists, repeatedly carry out gang rape for days and weeks on end and employ torture and reproductive harm to sterilize victims during rape.[104]

A year later, in mid-2022, as the Ethiopian war resumed after a short truce broke down, UN researchers documented Ethiopian government male soldiers forcing captured Tigray women into "sexual slavery."[105]

∽

Men's sexual assaults on women occur in several different militarized sites. In each, there are specific politics of masculinities at work, among both the rapists and among their superiors.[106] There is "rape in the ranks": male soldiers sexually assaulting women (and some men) among their own comrades.[107] There are also men's rapes of women as political prisoners at the command of militarized officials, as part of a state regime of torture. Chilean feminist anthropologist Ximena Bunster, investigating the gender dynamics of the Pinochet military junta, provides a documented account of rape of women prisoners as a masculinized weapon of militarized torture.[108]

Then there are systematic rapes of captured women by militarized men in what have been called "rape camps." Two feminist lawyers – friends since childhood in Bosnia, Jadranka Cigelj and Nusreta Sivac – were among the first to publicly describe their experiences in such Serbian-organized detention centers. They are at the center of a documentary film, *Calling the Ghosts*.[109] The Japanese Imperial Army's World War II Asia-wide system of "comfort women" brothels, organized to sexually serve Japanese male soldiers, has been categorized by Asian feminists as simply another system of rape camps. Korean, Filipino, Japanese and Taiwanese feminists have built alliances to support the now-elderly women survivors of these wartime so-called "brothels" as they have traveled to tell their stories.[110]

The rapes most widely reported have been male soldiers' sexual assaults on women that have been integrally woven into their battlefield operations, such as those documented by Dyan Mazurana and other feminist human rights researchers.

∽

As frequent and as varied as men's sexual assaults on women have been during so many armed conflicts, they have been hard to see, much less prosecute, because so much of war's waging has been shrouded in what has been called "the fog of war." Together, "fog of war" and "collateral damage" act as patriarchal bookends: they obfuscate what goes on in war. Of course, much of war is conducted in broad daylight. But describing war's setting as fog-shrouded leaves us with the mind-dulling impression that what happens during war is so chaotic, so confusing that we shouldn't even try to map the actions of soldiers or document the decisions made by those who deploy them.

"Fog of war" is the perfect stage set for impunity. Who can be held accountable if it is impossible to see what is going on?

Among the most important witnesses to what goes on in war are journalists. A skilled journalist can help blow away the fog of war. Until recently, most journalists covering wars were men. The masculinization of militaries seemed to have required the masculinization of war correspondents.

Publishers and editors are the people who decide which reporters to assign to which stories. For generations, those news executives were men who believed that only men could cover war – manly men, who could earn the trust of hardened frontline soldiers, live with rats in muddy trenches, go for days without a shower, take notes under fire, witness bloody wounds and drink their liquor with the other manly male war correspondents.

The masculinization of war journalism began to be challenged during World War II. Among the pioneers were three American professional journalists, Ruth Cowan, Martha Gellhorn and Dickey Chapelle. As described by Japanese Canadian documentary filmmaker Michèle Midori Fillion, the three women devised strategies for overcoming the opposition of their sexist editors and sexist wartime military commanders, none of whom believed women could or should be at the front as war correspondents. Fillion's documentary, *No Job for a Woman: The Women Who Fought to Report WWII*, shows how and with what results the three honed their distinct strategies to defy the media's sexism: "drink the guys under the table," "play up to the generals" or "find your stories behind the lines."[111]

The seemingly least aggressive of these strategies may have had the longest lasting effect on what we learn about war in the midst of war. To overcome the obstacles confronting women journalists during World War II, they decided to turn hospitals and the home front into news sites. To do that, they had to persuade their skeptical editors that such feminized spaces were among the places where wars should be covered.

Despite these pioneering journalists' considerable successes, though, war still continued to be imagined by editors, generals and most civilian readers as out of bounds for women journalists.

That masculinization of war coverage helped to sustain the fog of war.

Even if some male reporters – and their editors – were fiercely independent and wrote bitingly critical stories that made commanders and their political superiors grind their teeth, manly-men-among-manly-men was not an environment that provoked the sharpest journalistic insights. If, added to that, most of the male journalists shared the same ethnic or racial identities as the male rank and file soldiers, colonels and generals they were covering, crucial dynamics that shaped a conflict were likely to be missed. What seemed to these journalists to be merely "normal" would not look newsworthy.

By the time of the US-led war in Vietnam, from 1965–75, more women journalists – both reporters and photographers – were pressing to be assigned to the battlefront. One of the consequences of the reporting from those women on wartime Vietnam was that there were more intimate stories and more attention devoted to Vietnamese soldiers.[112] This was a decade in which women in many countries were organizing to break down the sexist doors of media companies. The masculinization of covering wars, national security, professional male sports, the financial industry and national elections was being challenged by women in the media.[113]

Women pursuing professional careers in news journalism recognized the benefits of making it to the war zone. The militarization of the civilian media meant that those journalists who were assigned to cover a war were accorded special importance in the industry: you were demonstrating physical bravery, you were where the action was, you were covering what *mattered*. British journalist Wendy Holden of London's *Daily Telegraph* described the attraction. She was returning from covering British military operations during the war in Iraq:

> You're suddenly a big cheese. Max Hastings [Editor-in-chief of the *Daily Telegraph*] would have me picked up at the airport to dine off drippy beef and claret with the great and the good, then I'd be dispatched to appear on [the BBC's] *Woman's Hour*.[114]

Despite these significant advances by women in war journalism, women as civilians trying to survive in war zones remained scarcely visible on the front pages of national papers or on primetime news programs. The central subjects of war coverage continued to be men. To cover war is to cover men.

Nonetheless, more women were becoming professional journalists *in* conflict areas. Among those women journalists were Arab women. With their language skills and their local connections – and their personal stakes in revealing the complexities of local politics – they reported on the Arab Spring and the militarized responses to those pro-democracy protest movements. Egyptian journalist Lina Attalah challenged the older men who ran the Egyptian news outlets she worked for to take seriously the young pro-democracy activists. Jane Arraf, a Canadian Palestinian, was assigned to Iraq during that country's war and sought to provide information for Iraqi women in households subjected to American soldiers' terrifying midnight house raids. For Bint el-Balad, a Syrian-born journalist whose childhood had been spent in several different Middle Eastern countries, reporting on Syria's post-2011 war brought the realization that her Syrian roots gave her higher stakes in covering this war than she first had imagined.[115]

There are still industry incentives for women journalists, as well as their male colleagues, to treat men as soldiers and men as politicians as the "real story" of any war. After all, the masculinization of both the media and war have not evaporated. The process of masculinization shrinks a journalist's curiosity and narrows the journalist's definition of what and who counts in war as "newsworthy." In so doing, masculinization helps to generate the "fog of war."

Something else has been shifting in the gendered dynamics of war reporting. Not only have more women been serving as war correspondents, more of those women journalists have been treating both civilian women's experiences in conflict zones and local women's ideas about war as newsworthy. Between 2001 and 2021, for instance, scores of Afghan women became professional news reporters covering their own country's long war. Afghan women studied journalism at university, ran radio stations, worked as journalists for both local and international newspapers, launched news sites on the web. Significantly, topics of their news coverage included Afghan women's daily lives and civil-society organizing. When the patriarchal men of the Taliban took power in August 2021, among their first moves was to oust women from media organizations. According to a joint report by the Afghan Independent Journalists Association and Reporters Without Borders, by December 2021, four out of five Afghan women in professional media jobs had been fired.[116]

Worldwide, the current generation of women journalists is more likely than their predecessors to have absorbed a feminist dual understanding: women's lives are interesting, and women have ideas worth listening to.

Journalist Sabrina Tavernise reflected this emerging dual understanding when she persuaded her *New York Times* editor in 2003 that spending a day in a modest women's beauty salon in the middle of Baghdad would afford her useful insights into Iraqis' reactions to the American army's arrival in the country's capital. There, as the lights flickered and the water flowed sporadically from the faucets, Tavernise listened to Iraqi women assessing their own wartime insecurity and the insecurity of their school-aged daughters. Women customers talked to Nimo, the owner, and exchanged information with each other about what to take into account as they made their daily security calculations. Maternal protection of teenage girls was a wartime topic being discussed in a safe all-women's space while getting one's hair washed.[117]

Security as understood and as strategically calculated by women and girls in a war zone: that has become newsworthy when journalists, informed by a feminist curiosity, weigh who is worth listening to during wartime.

∽

"We had to stay up after midnight there in those Rome hotels. If that meant drinking scotch in a delegate's room at 2am, we did it."

I was listening to a feminist recalling what it was like to be an activist in Rome in 1998. Government delegations had gathered in Rome to hammer out the fine print of what would become the Rome Statute.[118] This was the international treaty that would determine what and who the newly created international permanent war crimes tribunal – the International Criminal Court (the ICC), as it is formally known – could prosecute. Since the 1990s, a transnational network of feminists had been paying close attention to experiences of women in the former Yugoslavia and Rwanda (and to the international trials of accused war criminals in each). They had been informed too by feminists who had supported the former so-called Asian "comfort women." Together, these transnational feminist researchers, lawyers and activists realized that, despite the draft treaty's esoteric legal language, the stakes for women in these Rome negotiations were high. Would systematic wartime rape continue to be treated as a subcategory of war crimes and as merely a "crime of honor?" Would women's wartime forced marriages, forced abortions and forced births be prosecutable? Would women survivors get the sort of protection they would need if they were to appear as witnesses in a war crime trial?

The fact that the ICC Rome Statute's final provisions are as realistic as they are about what sorts of sexualized abuses so many women endure during wars is due to the determined application of gritty gender knowledge and determined feminist legal expertise, galvanized by activists prowling the hotel corridors after midnight in Rome in 1998.

Not all governments have ratified the Rome Statute. As of 2023, among the prominent holdouts were the governments of the US, Russia, China, Israel and Qatar. The ICC answers to the UN Security Council, and yet three of the Security Council's powerful five veto-wielding states have refused to join the ICC.

The feminist organizing that helped shape the fine print of the Rome Statute has continued. The organization for the monitoring of the ICC is Women's Initiatives for Gender Justice. It operates in The Hague to closely monitor the day-to-day workings of the ICC. Its staff members use feminist curiosity and feminist analytical skills to keep track of the priorities and practices of the ICC's investigators, prosecutors and judges.

Fine print in any treaty is hard to infuse with feminist understanding. Even when inserted, it takes continued organizing to ensure its faithful implementation.[119]

∽

Silencing women has been crucial to the underestimation of men's sexual assaults on women in wartime. Over the past fifty years, feminists who have campaigned against all forms of violence against women – domestic violence, sex trafficking, workplace sexual harassment, forced girlhood marriage, rape – have made challenging the politics of silencing central to their activism.

The girls and women who have remained silent about the violence they endure at the hands of many sorts of men have not been merely unthinkingly passive. Feminists do not blame the silenced. Rather, they try to understand what conditions make a woman choose silence. Feminists have learned to see that women and girls who have endured any kind of violence have made conscious decisions, even if they have had to make those decisions in the narrowest of social spaces. These women who have chosen silence have weighed their options, calculated the consequences, assessed the costs.

A major effort of women's anti-violence activists in scores of countries, therefore, has been to widen those girls' and women's options, to lessen the intimidating repercussions they face when speaking up, to build more trusting relationships with possible listeners and to provide genuine security for those who do choose to speak out. This is labor-intensive political work. Ask any volunteer who has worked at her local rape crisis center.

Since the 1980s, transnational feminist anti-violence activism has become part of international politics. Women's advocates have lobbied the United Nations, the European Union, the Council of Europe, Human Rights Watch, the World Health Organization, the International Committee of the Red Cross, the International Labor Organization, the International Union for the Conservation of Nature, the World Wildlife Fund and the World Bank to take seriously the causes and consequences of men's violence against women and to take explicit institutional actions to prevent it. That is why, for instance, the passage of the Council of Europe's Istanbul Convention in 2012 was so significant: it made prevention of violence against women a Europe-wide commitment.

That, in turn, is why the Hungarian government's refusal to ratify the Istanbul Convention, the Turkish government's withdrawal from the Istanbul Convention and the Ukrainian government's belated signing on to the Istanbul Convention – each in the midst of war – are so newsworthy. Women who endure sexual violence during war face added pressures to stay silent, because skeptics can weaponize their shaming efforts by implying that those women who were raped were willingly collaborating with the enemy. Alternatively, women sexually assaulted can face silencing disbelief or trivialization: "Deal with it yourself. Don't you realize there's a war on?"

∽

Feminist investigators establishing that "systematic wartime rape" has occurred or that rape has been wielded as "a weapon of war" depend on women survivors finding the courage and support to talk to trusted investigators about their ordeals in painful detail.

Each of these two concepts, however, is feminist *only* if it is employed in ways that take women survivors seriously and, in so doing, treat women survivors with care and dignity. That calls for patience. In wartime, urgency often trumps patience.

Holly Porter, a feminist anthropologist researching rural Ugandan women's experiences of rape during the protracted armed conflict in Northern Uganda, learned to slow down, way down. She refused to squeeze a woman into the narrow category that was her "research topic." Instead, she took a genuine interest in each Ugandan woman's full, complex life. She did not rush. It can take hours, weeks, months, she knew, to build trust; sometimes, the trust never comes. Holly learned to sit for hours with local women shelling ground nuts, taking part in the leisurely banter (in Acholi) of women working among women. Some days the talk turned to wartime experiences. Most days it didn't. Patience is respectful. Patience is a feminist investigatory skill to hone even while, as a feminist, one is impatient to redress patriarchal wrongs.[120]

"Systematic wartime rape" and "rape as a weapon of war" are concepts developed by feminists to provide us with a more realistic sense of warfare and with the vision to pursue accountability and justice. But each concept can be turned into an instrument of patriarchy if either is wielded by racists or war-wagers simply to objectify women as victims in pursuit of mobilizing hatred, revenge and further militarization. Post-civil war African American feminist campaigner and investigator Ida B Wells repeatedly warned against white male leaders of Jim Crow lynch mobs exploiting white women's alleged victimhood.[121] Three generations later, in 1975, Susan Brownmiller raised a similar warning flag: stories of sexual assaults on women could be turned into ideological ammunition for warmongers.[122]

Generations of feminists have learned never to underestimate the agility of those determined to sustain patriarchy. They will seek to turn even feminist ideas and feminist-informed policies into instruments for sustaining masculinized privilege.

That is why feminist anti-rape activists – in "peacetime" and wartime – have become so determined to give voice to rape survivors. They are not mere victims. They are not justifications for someone else's revenge. They are not simply witnesses for the prosecution. Survivors' own diverse understandings, their myriad wishes, their dissimilar recovery strategies have become central to many countries' anti-rape feminist movements. In rape crisis shelters, in #MeToo campaigns and in wartime feminist-informed humanitarian aid programs it takes a special commitment to the well-being of survivors to allow their voices to be heard, their wishes to be respected. Their goals and priorities may diverge from those of their dedicated supporters. Rape survivors may not prioritize successful war crimes trials in The Hague. They may not choose to be interviewed by even respectful journalists or committed war crimes investigators. They may not place justice at the center of their own healing.

Or they may.

∽

Four women were sitting together in a small kitchen. Lace curtains were pulled across the window, potted plants lined the sill.[123] The women were sitting in Olha's house in the southern Ukrainian town of Kherson. It was several weeks after the Ukrainian military had driven occupying Russian soldiers out of Kherson. Olha chose to give only her first name.

One of the four women there in Olha's kitchen was Anna Sosonska. She was a Ukrainian war crimes investigator sent from the prosecutor general's office in Kyiv. Olha had agreed to speak to her about her ordeal during the Russian occupation. The other two women sitting with Olha and Anna were American journalists – a reporter and a photographer. Olha had agreed for them to join the conversation, though with conditions. It was too soon, she had decided, to take the chance of being widely recognized. What if some of her socially conservative neighbors stigmatized her as a tainted woman, or even blamed her for what the soldiers had done to her? And what if the Russian soldiers returned?

In response to Anna Sosonska's questions, Olha described what she had experienced at the hands of the occupying Russian soldiers. She was a twenty-six-year-old civilian woman living in the port town of Kherson. Russian soldiers had forcibly detained her. One day, after being held a week, Russian soldiers tied her to a table. They pulled off her clothes below her waist. As she lay there, tied to the table and half-naked, the lead interrogator called her vile names for fifteen minutes. He then threw a jacket over her, stalked out and let seven other Russian men into the room. As Olha remembered, "It was to frighten . . . I did not know what would come next."

After listening to Olha's account, Anna Sosonska, the Ukrainian woman serving as a war crimes investigator, said that Olha's ordeal confirmed what other Ukrainian women had told her of their experiences of sexual abuse while held in detention: "We are finding this problem of sexual violence in every place that Russia occupied . . . Every place: Kyiv region, Chernihiv region, Kharkiv region, Donetsk region and also here in Kherson." Her findings revealed a pattern. It revealed a "system."

The photographer asked Olha if she could take her picture. Olha agreed, though she said the picture must not reveal her face. She got up and went to the kitchen window. She pulled back the lace curtain slightly and faced outward. The back she showed to the photographer was straight.

∽

Sohaila Abdulali, the Indian US feminist writer, activist and rape survivor, offers a feminist caution:

> It's quite a balancing act – you don't want to have a secret you can't share, but you equally don't want this one thing that happened to you to be the biggest thing on everyone's mind when they think of you. I hope being a rape survivor isn't the most interesting thing about me or anyone else.[124]

EIGHT

Feminists Organize While War Is Raging

THE AUDITORIUM WAS ALMOST full; the atmosphere was tense. No one knew if government agents were in the room.

This was Istanbul, 2009.

Ayşe Gül Altinay, a Turkish feminist scholar and activist, had invited me to take part in this historic gathering. Outside the hall, Istanbul's magnificent mosques remained unscathed. There were no soldiers on the city's streets or screeches of incoming artillery missiles overhead. Yet this was wartime. Young men were being conscripted into the government's military and deployed to a war zone. Civilians living in Turkey's south-east region were trying to survive amidst ongoing clashes between the government's powerful military and Kurdish insurgent militias.

A coalition of Turkish activists had organized this Istanbul meeting to support those Turkish men who were refusing to fulfill their compulsory military service. They had invited activist conscientious objectors from several countries outside Turkey to take part. In countries such as Germany, Sweden, the US, Canada and Argentina, at that time – at least in theory (far harder in practice) – a man could formally appeal to be exempted from compulsory military service once he was officially recognized as a conscientious objector. In Turkey – as in Russia and South Korea, as well as in Eritrea and Israel (both of which have compulsory military service for both women and men) – conscientious objection had no legal standing.

In the years after this Istanbul gathering, the issue of conscientious objection would become more widely salient, because in 2021 Norway and Sweden reintroduced military conscription – for both women and men – though, in practice, only on a highly selective basis.[125]

Feminists have learned that the politics of masculinities are always in play not only around men's conscription, but also men's claims of conscientious objection. Members of the public have lent their support to the policy of compulsory male military service by ridiculing young men who seek CO status. "Conchie" was a derogatory British term hurled at COs during both World War I and II. A "conchie" was not just a man who claimed that his conscience prohibited him from engaging in warfare. He also was, allegedly, a man who refused to be properly manly. Consequently, it has taken confidence in one's moral order – often anchored in religious belief (many British and North American CO claimants have been Quakers) – and in one's own alternative form of masculinity for any individual man to go through the elaborate bureaucratic process of seeking CO status, especially if one's country is at war.

Among the central organizers of the Istanbul gathering were Turkish feminists. Many of them opposed their government's ongoing war in the south-east against the country's Kurdish minority. Supporting those few men taking the risk of refusing to fulfill their military service obligations seemed part and parcel of their feminist opposition to militarism, and to their support of Kurdish minority rights.

The political alliance, however, wasn't as natural as it may have seemed. Turkish feminists did not want to be part of a political process – even a quite daring, oppositional process – that confirmed men as political heroes.[126]

These Turkish activist women had become all too aware that even anti-war, anti-military social movements can slide into patriarchal ways of mobilizing, ways that presume women's supportive subordination. Who are the movement's presumed leaders? Whose strategic or tactical decisions are accorded the most weight? What sorts of symbolic acts are deemed central to the movement's public demonstrations? Who in the peace movement sleeps with whom – with what consequences for each? Who serves the coffee? Whose individual actions are imagined by other activists to be "heroic"? The answers given to each of these questions can tip an opposition social movement into patriarchy.

Many women have come to their own feminism by beginning to ask these awkward questions while engaged in social justice, anti-colonial, anti-racist and anti-war movements. Their feminist questioning has not always been welcomed by their fellow activists.[127]

Turkish feminists had carved out space in this meeting to pose questions about heroism. The male COs – who were indeed risking arrest by appearing there in a public space – had realized that the gendered questions asked by their feminist supporters were legitimate.

Some Turkish feminists wanted to push even further. Ferda Ülker and a handful of women from the coastal city of Izmir had been talking among themselves about their roles in their country's militarization. They had concluded that the male-only character of the state's military conscription law should not limit who could publicly declare themselves to be "conscientious objectors."

The Turkish feminist declaration of conscientious objection to militarism caused a buzz at the Istanbul gathering. Everyone started talking about what exactly any Turkish woman could refuse to do to avoid complicity in their government's militarism and its offensives against Kurdish insurgents. Women would become actors, not just men's supporters.

Ferda Ülker's statement read in part:

Militarism is always like an unannounced and shameless guest in every aspect of life, especially for women living in this geography: in the streets, at home, at work, in our fields of struggle, and everywhere . . .

I declare that today, as much as before, I shall defy every secret and obvious form of militarism and show solidarity with anyone who defies militarism . . .

I REJECT![128]

⁓

Week after week, Belgrade Women in Black stood out in the busy traffic intersection of Serbia's capital, in the midst of a brutal ethno-nationalist war, holding up signs demanding: "No War," "Stop Rape Now." This was dangerous. Yet they continued their protests.

Syrian women, under the cover of homeschooling, taught young boys and their mothers that fighting was not manly. This was risky in a wartime village where military and militia recruiters were forcing boys to take up arms. But they did it.

Afghan women – dozens of them – ran for parliamentary office in the middle of a war that had, as one of its central debates, the question of whether women should be visible in public life. Despite facing threats of assassination, and against wartime odds, some of them won their legislative seats. One of them, Fawzia Koofi, would rise to the post of deputy speaker of the Afghan Parliament. Not surprisingly, when the Taliban regained power in August 2021, these women MPs became targets for oppression. Their post-war would be spent in exile or in hiding.[129]

Kurdish women organized autonomously against domestic violence while their south-eastern Turkish city of Diyarbakir was under siege. It sounded like madness. But the Kurdish Turkish women who organized KAMER did it. Their women-run restaurants even dared to have glass windows.[130]

There are many current and recent examples of women's ingenuity, but feminist organizing in the midst of war is not new. What *is* new is our recognition of – and our drawing lessons from – feminist wartime organizing and strategizing, past and present.

∽

1915. The war was supposed to have been "over by Christmas." Instead, it was in its second bloody year. Greenish clouds of poison gas were floating over the French trenches. Ottoman troops were forcing thousands of ethnic Armenians to march to their deaths. Allied soldiers had begun their landings at Gallipoli. Patriotic fervor was rising among optimistic Britons. A German submarine had sunk a passenger liner, the *Lusitania,* during its Atlantic crossing, drowning 1,198 civilians.

This was not a good time for women to be crossing oceans and state boundaries to convene a meeting in the Netherlands.

And yet, 1,200 women converged on The Hague in April 1915 to hold the world's first Women's Peace Congress. The American delegates had come by ship, the *Noordam,* defying the German U-boats. Scandinavian delegates had come by ship and train; the Dutch, Belgian, Austrian, Hungarian, German, Italian and Polish women had journeyed across war zones by train. British Foreign Office officials were unhappy when they heard that 180 British women delegates were on their way to cross the English Channel to attend the Congress. The officials denied the women's passport applications and stopped the channel ferries. The Minister of Munitions, Winston Churchill, labeled the congress delegates "these dangerous women." Three British women did make it to The Hague, either by being already there as part of the organizing committee or traveling with the Americans.[131]

Most of the thousand-plus women who made it to The Hague had been doing local suffrage campaigning work before the war and had networked through the International Women's Suffrage Alliance. The outbreak of war provoked intense discussions among suffragists about the political and personal relationships between women's rights and waging war.

Before 1914, many suffragists, though not all, identified as pacifists. Should suffragists, as British militant suffragist Emmeline Pankhurst urged, now throw themselves into war work to prove to skeptical men that women's skills were valuable for national defense and that suffragists were true patriots? Or, contrarily, should suffragists stand by their conviction that war was a patriarchal endeavor that simply sent the roots of masculinized privilege deeper into a nation's soil?

Millicent Fawcett, another leading British suffragist, was torn. She saw the strategic value of suffragists openly supporting the government's war effort, yet to do so would violate her own pacifist convictions. Suffrage activists with whom Fawcett worked in the

English university town of Cambridge angrily split. Some prioritized their anti-war principles. Others volunteered for war work.[132]

These debates, and the painful ambivalence felt by many women activists with the explosion of war in 1914, will sound familiar to most women's rights activists today. They should. The complex dynamics between patriotism, support for a nation's or community's armed defense, anti-violence activism, militarism and patriarchy are never easy for feminists to negotiate.[133]

This makes feminist anti-militarist organizing a perpetual work-in-progress. Absorbing that hard reality still requires a special sort of political stamina.

It was the Dutch feminist Aletta Jacobs who formally invited women to come to an international congress. The women who filled The Hague's Peace Palace in April 1915 came from a range of social classes in their own countries, and from both antagonistic belligerent nations and neutral nations. Jane Addams, famous both for her suffrage campaigning and her social work with poor and immigrant women in Chicago, was elected the president of the Congress.

The wartime narrative exerted intense public pressures on each woman to see herself solely in terms of narrow patriotism – acting as though the women from rival states were her enemies. The women who met in The Hague withstood those pressures on women to distrust each other and, instead, chose to see themselves as bonded together by their twinned convictions: first, that women had valuable ideas to contribute to the understanding both of war's *causes* and *conclusions* and, second, that the current destructive war had to be ended as quickly as possible.

"When do you suppose the big row will come off?" asked a New York journalist. Up in the press gallery, the male reporters looked down at the assembly of women. It was an unusual sight; it could be hardly serious, they imagined, scarcely credible. Surely, the women would "row." And women going after one another was so entertaining.

A less patronizing male reporter, sitting nearby, was covering the Congress for a magazine called *The Advocate for Peace.* He recorded his amusement at his fellow reporter's lazy assumption: "My New York colleague left in disgust on the third day of the conference because his hopes to witness some sensational outburst or manifestation of hysteria were sorely disappointed."[134]

The Congress's thousand women delegates drafted and passed twenty resolutions. Looking forward to what today is being conceptualized as "feminist foreign policy," their resolutions spelled out in detail what a just, sustainable peace would look like and, consequently, what needed to be included in any meaningful peace settlement. Their resolutions also considered process. Resolution 8: "Democratic Control of Foreign Policy"; Resolution 9: "The Enfranchisement of Women."[135]

Before they adjourned to make their perilous journeys home, the Congress women formed two small delegations to take their resolutions to all the governments of Europe, to present their case for ending the war and for creating a just, inclusive, sustainable peace. Words, they knew, were never enough. The Congress had to be followed up with organized action.

◠

Out of the historic Women's Peace Congress came The Women's International League for Peace and Freedom (WILPF), which today remains engaged in local and international feminist peace campaigning. In April 2015, when hundreds of women activists again descended on The Hague to celebrate WILPF's centenary, the forty-one country delegations represented far more of the world's women than they had at its initial gathering. There were now delegations from Serbia, Ukraine, Mexico, Chad, India, Afghanistan and Pakistan. Nigeria's WILPF leader, Joy Onyesoh, and Liberian feminist Nobel Peace Prize laureate Leymah Gbowee gave keynote speeches. Delegates from the newly organized Cameroon and Ghana sections took part. A Japanese delegate was elected WILPF's new president.[136]

The atmosphere at the centenary was not merely celebratory. In 2015, most of the women were engaging in feminist activism in countries at war or in countries whose governments were contributing to wars elsewhere. The stakes were high. Exposing and challenging the causal relationships between militarism and patriarchy remained at the center of WILPF's mission. Nevertheless, WILPF's activists returned to their home countries to confront quite distinct local militarizing sexist conditions.

As during the earlier suffrage wartime era, forging feminist international solidarity meant remaining respectful of localized workings of patriarchy and militarism.

For instance, women active in the Cameroon WILPF section, led by Sylvie Ndongmo, tracked their own government's increasing autocracy, which they understood to be only fueling societal tensions. Under these conditions, they decided, preventing local inter-communal violence between their country's Francophone and Anglophone speakers required urgent trust-building. When, during the 2020 global Covid pandemic, public health became a local priority, Ndongmo and her fellow feminist peace activists decided that building trust across Cameroon's mutually suspicious communities could be achieved only by treating feminist local activism, women's security, regional peacebuilding and fact-based public health education as mutually reinforcing.

A year later, Cameroonian feminists joined with women from eighteen other African WILPF country sections and groups to write a joint regional report. In it, they called on the region's male-dominated governments to stop justifying their shrinkage of civil-society space in the name of fighting extremism. They demanded women local activists be included in security and health decision-making. They additionally insisted that prevention of violence against women (which was escalating during the Covid pandemic lockdowns) be considered integral to establishing genuine national security.

As Sylvie Ndongmo concluded, "We are clearheaded."[137]

Sweden's WILPF activists had lent African WILPF women logistical support so they could hold their regional meetings and publish their feminist pandemic report. It felt to the Swedish feminists as though they were doing the sort of transnational feminist peace work they were especially equipped to do.

Just a year later, however, these same Swedish feminists felt compelled to focus most of their energies on slowing down Sweden's own galloping militarization.[138]

Swedish feminists have tried for years to dispel the popular international myth that Sweden was pacifistic. They repeatedly explained that being neutral in international rivalries was not synonymous with pacifism. In reality, Sweden had a sizable military and a significant arms industry, led by the fighter-plane manufacturer, Saab. In recent years, furthermore, the Swedish government had introduced military conscription for both women and men, and had forged ever-closer relations with NATO, sending troops to Afghanistan, even if not formally joining the military alliance.

Sweden's 2014–19 foreign minister, Margot Wallström, made popular the concept of a "feminist foreign policy," an approach that prioritized women's rights, human rights, peace and equitable development. It was no coincidence that Wallström came to her Swedish cabinet post from service as the UN Special Representative on Sexual Violence in Conflict. She also had been in close contact with Swedish feminist groups such as WILPF-Sweden and Kvinna till Kvinna. She knew how vital commitment to women's rights was to an entire government foreign policy.

Inspired by Wallström, the Canadian, German and Mexican governments announced that they too would adopt a feminist foreign policy, though some of their own women's civil-society groups were skeptical. Those groups have continued to develop the concept, making ever clearer what a genuine feminist foreign policy would look like in practice.[139]

When she tried to apply feminist peace commitments to Sweden's trade agreements with Saudi Arabia, Margot Wallström got public pushback from Saab. Other Swedish companies, including non-military firms such as the global apparel brand H&M, joined Saab in arguing that any restrictions on the export of Swedish products hurt all Swedish companies. Wallström resigned her cabinet post, though she continued to be an advocate for feminist foreign policy.[140]

Russia's invasion of Ukraine in February 2022 had a major impact on Swedish feminist peace activism. On top of that shock (and not unrelated), came the Swedish national parliamentary elections, which gave the center-right party coalition the power to govern. One of the

new cabinet's first steps was to publicly discard any Swedish commitment to a "feminist foreign policy."

How could Swedish feminist peace activists spell out their support
for Ukrainians, while still working to slow down Sweden's own militarization, when those militarizing policies were being justified as
solidarity with Ukraine, as well as defense of Sweden against the
threat of Putin's aggression?

Swedish feminist peace activists never had been sanguine about
their influence in the country's political affairs. They had had access
to government ministers, such as Foreign Minister Margot Wallström,
so long as the Social Democrats were in office. They knew that many
Swedish officials enjoyed Sweden having the international reputation
of being a "gender equal society": it was good for the country's
"brand."[141] But they never fooled themselves into imagining that they
exercised real political clout or that they could relax their feminist
scrutiny of the government. Now, in the aftermath of Russia's invasion
of Ukraine, and in the wake of voters tilting right, there was the risk
of Swedish feminist peace activists being pushed further to the political margins, as their fellow citizens contracted the militarism fever
and rallied around NATO membership.

As both Cameroonian and Swedish feminist peace activists organized to push back local militarizations, they acted as partners in
transnational efforts to craft and enact a global feminist anti-war agenda.
They paid attention to the United Nations. WILPF's central office in
Geneva had created a small branch in New York, just across First
Avenue from the UN headquarters, to help co-ordinate feminist local/
transnational campaigns – against wartime sexual violence, against the
international gun trade, against nuclear weapons, for gender-informed
climate security, for reproductive health, for sexual rights. Local feminist organizing and global feminist organizing have to be in constant
touch with each other. That takes a special sort of political stamina.[142]

⁓

Since October 2000, those feminist peace campaigns have been
framed by UN Security Council Resolution (UNSCR) 1325 on

Women, Peace and Security. While it – and follow-up resolutions, all pushed by feminist peace activist groups – is formal UN policy, the rationale for – the ground-up knowledge informing – and the very wording of "1325" were the result of a historic alliance between women civil-society activists and feminist civil servants working inside UN agencies, such as the UN Development Program's women's program ("UNIFEM," which later morphed into UN Women).

Among the civil society organizations whose feminist-informed staff contributed to 1325 were WILPF, MADRE, Human Rights Watch, Amnesty International, Rutgers University's Center for Women's Global Leadership, the International Committee of the Red Cross and Oxfam. There was nothing "automatic" about such an alliance. It had grown out of increasing numbers of feminists working inside each of these organizations sharing information with each other. Moreover, there was no guarantee, even in the wake of documented widespread rapes in Rwanda and Bosnia, that the state delegates sitting around the table of the Security Council – at the pinnacle of the UN's structural hierarchy – would consider, much less pass, the drafted resolution. After all, in its seventy-five years of existence, the Security Council never before passed a resolution devoted to the rights and well-being of women in war.

"UNSCR 1325" stands on two pillars of understanding, each infused with knowledge gained over the past thirty years by local feminists working in societies plagued by armed conflict. The first pillar: that women's experiences of war, especially as victims and survivors of men's wartime sexual violence, must be recognized and explicitly addressed by national and international political decision makers. The second pillar: that every ceasefire, peace agreement and post-war recovery plan must be negotiated with meaningful participation from women in civil society.

"We ran from the Security Council back to the office, turned on our fax machine and began sending 1325 to every feminist group in the world we knew!"

This was Felicity Ruby (then Felicity Hill), an Australian feminist staff member of Women's International League for Peace and Freedom, recalling the excitement she and her fellow feminists felt when, on October 1, 2000, the delegates of the UN Security Council passed UNSCR 1325. The feminists' excitement was not simply in getting the Security Council on record as taking women's wartime conditions seriously. Rather, their excitement was in being able to provide a new tool for local women activists in war zones.[143]

In the almost twenty-five years since the Security Council's remarkable passage of 1325, local feminists from Yemen, Congo and Sudan to Afghanistan, Syria and Colombia have used its provisions to press their national officials and myriad international actors (including influential donors) to implement both key commitments. It has been rough going. Local male elites and international agency men keep prioritizing their relationships with each other. Many of them are afraid that, if they start insisting on women's rights, the conservative militarized men will shut off communication. Better, those men say, to keep channels open between the men who matter. Women's rights, women's care, women's participation can come later.

Held up as a shining example of 1325's positive impact has been the 2016 "Havana Peace Accord," which ended the conflict between the Colombian government and its military and the armed militias of the insurgent FARC. The Havana Accord included several explicit provisions for women survivors of sexual violence, women as land holders and women as political participants. Behind that shining light, however, was Colombian women's own determined organizing.

At a breakfast meeting in Bogota in 2015, when the Havana negotiations were in progress and war continued to wreak havoc in women's and men's lives, twenty-five Colombian women activists sat around a table to strategize. They represented more than a dozen distinct Colombian women's groups – rural and urban, Black, mestizo and white, Catholic and secular. They did not agree on many things (abortion rights of wartime rape survivors was a sensitive topic). But they were realists; they had found ways to stick together to present a women's united front in the peace negotiations. They used the international commitments spelled out in 1325 to leverage their influence.[144]

∽

Some of the feminists monitoring 1325 became dismayed at the efforts of patriarchal states and patriarchal UN agencies to shrink and hollow out the feminist content of 1325. Those officials had initially resisted the adoption of 1325. Once 1325 was passed, these state and international actors set about limiting its practical effects on their own interests and practices.

These officials certainly did not want women civil-society activists – women who knew in detail the economic and physical realities misshaping the lives of women in war zones – to become real players in the high-stakes politics of peace negotiations and post-war reconstruction.[145]

Since its 2000 passage, officials resistant to the 1325 double mandate adopted a strategy of making women as victims more central to their own 1325 narratives and actions, rather than women as engaged political participants. The 1325-resisters then shrunk "participation" down to merely increasing women as uniformed personnel in military peacekeeping operations. Women as silent victims, women as rank-and-file soldiers. They were adapting, at least superficially, to today's international norms; patriarchal sustainers of masculinized privilege were learning how to digest both of the mandates of 1325 without surrendering much of their own power.

Transnational feminists weren't fooled. They had had decades of experience dealing with political elites who had learned to talk the talk without walking the walk. In conversation, Madeleine Rees, Secretary General of WILPF, and Joy Onyesoh, Nigerian peace activist and vice president of WILPF International, agreed that co-optation by cynical policy elites posed an ever-present danger to local peace activists. Nonetheless, because responsibility to protect human rights continues to be vested in states, feminists must keep finding ways to engage with state officials. They agreed, however, that the work that local women peace activists do on the ground was the most authentic form of peace building. As Joy Onyesoh explained:

> When you resolve conflicts that would otherwise escalate, you raise awareness about zero tolerance for violence, you raise awareness about discrimination, promote early responses to conflicts, and show that people can go about their lives without fear, that's a peace process.[146]

NINE

"Post-war" Can Last Generations

"LATER" IS A PATRIARCHAL time zone.

Feminists have learned this lesson the hard way. In the throes of war, many women have bitten their tongues and withheld their dissent, hoping their countries' male leaders would keep their promises that, when peace returned, their rights would be respected, their needs would be addressed.

"When the enemy has been defeated."

"When the revolution has succeeded."

"When the nation is secure."

"When the time is right."

Yet, when peace does come – or, at least, when the guns have gone silent – the overwhelming impulse is to return to normal. "Normal" is usually patriarchal.

Kuwaiti suffragists, however, were impatient. During the 1990–91 wartime occupation by Iraqi military, Kuwaiti women had joined the resistance. In the middle of what is now called the "First Gulf War," local women took care of the wounded, smuggled food and ammunition, passed on secret messages and hid Kuwaiti fighters. Once Saddam Hussein's Iraqi forces were defeated and expelled from Kuwait, these women expected to have their contributions to the nation's victory acknowledged by the men who controlled their monarchical state.

Kuwaiti suffragists refused to sit back and wait for men to act. They knew there would be nothing automatic about post-war recognition of the value of women to the nation. Suffragists would have to organize, exert pressure on the emir and the men in Kuwait's increasingly influential parliament. It took more than a decade of post-war non-violent organizing and protesting for Kuwaiti women suffragists to win the vote. When their victory came in 2005, it was called the "Blue Revolution."

Kuwaiti women ran for office, pressed for legal reform, urged that women be allowed to volunteer for the army and called on the government to prevent sexual harassment and reverse the male-dominated judiciary's lax punishments for men who murdered their wives or daughters in the name of preserving family "honor."

By 2022, socially conservative men dominated Kuwait's elected parliament. Seventeen years after winning the right to vote, women comprised a mere 6.25% of the parliament's members (four women among sixty men). The very success of the women's suffrage move-ment had galvanized Kuwait's most conservative men to organize electorally. With their new political leverage, they pushed back against women's post-war gains.

Still, Kuwaiti women's organizations proliferated; their public protests grew more vocal. As Najeeba Hayat, a co-founder of Kuwait's #MeToo movement, told women rallying outside the parliament in February 2022, "If there's a protest, I'm going to show up. If there's someone who needs convincing, I'm going to try."[147]

Kuwaiti women suffragists joined a long line of women's rights advocates who had resisted post-war efforts to "return to normal." In that line have been women in war-recovering countries as disparate as Italy, France, Japan, Britain, the Netherlands, the US, Canada, Germany, Greece, Turkey, Austria and Poland. In each, suffrage activists sought to convert women's wartime sacrifices and contribu-tions into expanded political rights. In the aftermath of World War I, Austrian and Polish women were the first of these to win – in November 1918 – the right to vote. Italian, French and Japanese women had to survive yet a second world war before they could win a "post-war" suffrage victory.[148]

As persuasive as it has been for post-war women campaigners to point to women's wartime contributions as the justification for women gaining the right to vote on the same terms as men, the strategy has come with a risk. Women (and the men supporting them) hanging their suffrage rights claims on women's actions in war risks militarizing women's citizenship: a woman is worthy of full citizenship status in so far as she proves her value in waging war. What is a woman's political worth if she works to prevent armed conflict, if she promotes anti-militarism?

Any post-war era lasts as long as we continue to draw lessons from it.

Over a century after the start of the post-World War I era, and over seventy-five years after the beginning of the post-World War II era, many of us are still drawing lessons from them. To the extent that we narrate any women's suffrage story as "women were given the vote because of their contribution to the war effort," we are militarizing women's rights and seriously underestimating women's pre-war and anti-war work in building an effective suffrage movement.

Do we give credit only to Emmeline Pankhurst, without talking about the 180 women British pacifist suffragists who tried to travel to The Hague in 1915? Do we explore Jane Addams's motivations for crossing the Atlantic in the midst of war or do we continue to valorize her mainly for her local social work achievements? When we tell the transnational story of women's suffrage, do we even mention Aletta Jacobs?

And then, of course, there is our choice of words. When we tell a suffrage story, do we say, "when women were *given* the vote"? If we do, we are continuing to ignore women's decades of pre-war, wartime and post-war campaigning, thereby bestowing credit for women's achievement of political rights on men in governments. Likewise, in telling the important stories of Turkish and Japanese women's suffrage, do we narrate those post-war stories in ways that turn senior military men – Kemal Atatürk and Douglas MacArthur – into the "givers" of women's suffrage. If we do, we turn generals into feminist heroes.

"Post-war" begins to fade when we critically reflect on those stories and begin to revise our narrations of women's post-war lives.

"Post-war" is not simply the months and years that sequentially follow war. That is, post-war is not just after war. Rather, "post-war" is an era that continues to be *defined by* a previous war. The US Civil War can still feel as though it is far from over. Mexico's 1910–17 revolutionary war was over issues – land, race – that are far from resolved. World War II remains relevant in the lives of many Koreans, Poles, Okinawans and Finns.[149]

In a society whose women and men are living in a post-war era, the material, psychological and cultural dynamics of war can remain salient. The hopes, stereotypes, narratives, hierarchies and fears that activated women and men in wartime don't simply evaporate when the peace agreement is signed. They morph, yet stay alive in minds and in policy justifications.

∽

That is why veterans are so politically important during post-war times. A veteran is defined in most countries as a person who has served in the uniform of a recognized fighting force. Which fighters wearing which uniforms during the recent war will count as post-war "veterans"? That is one of the issues that is hammered out by the people who obtain a seat at the peace negotiation table.[150]

Veterans typically are given post-war benefits, even if insufficient: hiring preferences, medical care priorities, education and training access, pensions. Those who will be registered as veterans are usually overwhelmingly male. Women who worked in wartime hospitals, who cared for wounded sons and husbands, who endured violence at the hands of emotionally disturbed veteran-husbands, who covered the war as journalists, who staffed government civilian offices, who protected museum's art works, who worked in munitions factories, who endured wartime injury and rape – they will not be registered as "veterans."

Nonetheless, even those women and girls who do manage to be registered as "veterans" are frequently marginalized.

Women and male veterans cope with dissimilar issues after wars. In the wake of the US war in Vietnam, American military nurses had to organize and exert pressure on the US government to compel the Department of Veterans' Affairs to admit that its hospitals were set up to serve only male veterans. First, they demanded that VA hospitals should add gynecological units. Later, during the US-led wars in Afghanistan and Iraq, American women veterans lobbied for the creation of special veterans' health clinics to address sexual trauma.

The men (and some women) who fill post-war policy posts are nervous about male veterans. If those men become disgruntled, they could cause trouble. True, post-war widows, if neglected, could embarrass the government. Yes, girls and women fighters who voluntarily leave the armed militias might make for unsightly post-war street scenes as they become homeless or work as prostitutes. But it is men as veterans who could cause serious trouble, perhaps violent trouble. Angry male veterans might be drawn into the illegal drug trade; they might form criminal gangs; they might "return to the bush" to join newly emergent militias; they might dig up the guns they buried to avoid post-war weapons confiscators.

Feminist researchers studying Liberia's gendered post-war politics have observed that local officials worried about the threats that male veterans could cause to the country's stability. International actors worried as well: "The international aid community thus became obsessed with the temporary removal of male idleness in Liberia."[151]

In the last two decades, nervous officials' nightmares informed many post-war recovery programs. Their anxieties, though, didn't inspire programs that actually provided most Liberian male veterans with decent employment, safe housing or a sense of social belonging. Rather, officials' worries led them to build demobilization programs that targeted male, not female, veterans.

"DDR" became the popular acronym for these post-war programs, most of which have been instituted in the Global South. DDR stands for Disarmament, Demobilization and Reintegration. The more local and international officials worried about "idle" male veterans, the more the programs prioritized the D and D, neglecting the R. The result: despite their pre-occupation with disgruntled male veterans, these officials (and their contractors) designed programs that scarcely addressed these men's post-war deeper hopes – hopes for steady waged jobs, secure housing and a desire to belong.[152]

Simultaneously, the proliferating DDR programs shut out women and girls who were being demobilized by armed groups. Gender advisors noticed the most glaring exclusionary practice: requiring guns. People running DDR camps realized that the benefits they were holding out to attract demobilized fighters would be attractive to almost anyone trying to piece together a life in a society impoverished by war: medical care, regular meals, counselling and job training. They needed to ensure that only "real" ex-fighters got through the gates. What would be credible evidence that a person was a deserving ex-fighter? Turning in a gun.

This simplistic organizational thinking revealed a dearth of gender curiosity about how fighting forces operated. Most girls and women who volunteered with, or were abducted into fighting forces were not issued guns. Girls and women played diverse roles as couriers, smugglers, nurses, launderers and enslaved "wives." When the peace agreement was signed and the DDR camps were created, the priority of many male commanders was to get their own male fighters access to the DDR benefits. Girls and women were simply dropped off the back of pick-up trucks in their home villages (many of whose residents did not trust or want them – or their children).[153]

Oretha was a veteran of a Liberian fighting force. She had washed male soldiers' clothes, bandaged them after battles, collected food for them. More than a decade later, Oretha (her wartime name) "hustled," making her precarious living on the streets of Monrovia, selling first sex, then drugs: "I never fought so I never disarmed. I only carried armor for them but I never fought. So how would I disarm?"[154]

∽

Post-war eras are shaped by feminized and masculinized silences. Male veterans don't admit to visiting wartime brothels or having nightmares of shooting unarmed civilians when staffing checkpoints. Some of those men might eventually break their silences, but many do not, fearing they will betray their wartime comrades or risk their status as patriots.[155]

Women also may live their post-war lives wrapped in protective silences. It is hard to admit anger at being left to carry the burdens of wartime single parenting. It can be dangerous to describe coerced wartime marriages. One can feel ashamed for surviving gang rape. Women's post-war eras continue as long as women remain afraid to break those feminized silences. When, decades later, some women do tell what happened to them – to a granddaughter, a therapist, a patient documentary filmmaker or a sensitive human rights researcher – the rest of their society may resist absorbing their long-buried truths.[156]

Post-war politics are also contests over memory: contests over who shapes which memories to create which lessons of war.[157]

Post-war inspires museums and monuments. Many celebrate victories and the victors, or validate the sacrifices of the defeated. They become part of a militarized war story. It can take years for a less triumphalist story to be told, a less celebratory museum to open, a more inclusive monument to be commissioned.[158] Monuments and museums devoted to women's wartime experiences come later, if at all. Their sponsors conduct fresh feminist-informed research, raise money from newly conscious donors and obtain the zoning permits.

Britain's Monument to the Women of World War II was dedicated at its prominent site on London's Whitehall in 2005, seventy years after the end of that war. The sculpture is a rendition in bronze of dozens of smocks belonging to women's munition factory workers, hanging on their workplace pegs.[159] The American monument recognizing the 11,000 American women military nurses who served during the US war in Vietnam took decades to fund. Designed by sculptor Glenna Goodacre, it was unveiled on the National Mall in 1993, just short of twenty years after the US withdrew its forces from Vietnam.[160]

In The Hague, a group monitoring the ICC's post-war prosecutions – Women's Initiatives for Gender Justice – created their own monument. In white tiles, the Gender Justice Legacy Wall celebrates

151 women and feminist groups who made significant contributions to the pursuit of post-war gender justice: individuals and groups who campaigned – often risking their own safety – against *impunity*. Impunity is a post-war plague. Impunity provides a peacetime cover for warlords and war criminals. Among the names chosen for the monument were those of African women judges who tried war criminals, Asian grassroots groups who broke silences to expose wartime crimes against women, as well as individual feminist anti-impunity researchers and activists across the world. The resultant Gender Justice Legacy Wall was erected in the lobby of the International Criminal Court in 2022.[161]

Museums are not just for the display and preservation of art; they are for learning – and unlearning. The stories they tell when they open may not be the stories they tell a generation later. As museum curators – and librarians – keep learning, captions under displays may be rewritten; new artifacts added; exhibits rearranged; new visitors attracted; once-featured items sent down to storage. To keep learning about past wars, to absorb their more useful lessons, one often needs to seek out the smallest post-war museums.

In Oslo, the Resistance Museum tells the story of Norwegian men and women who resisted the World War II Nazi occupation. Press a button to hear the recorded voice of Norwegian Nazi-collaborator prime minister Vidkun Quisling.

In Hong Kong, pro-democracy volunteers created a micro-museum to keep alive and visible the experiences of men and women arrested and killed by China's military in June 1989 for staging a pro-democracy rally in Beijing's Tiananmen Square. Hoping to be less vulnerable, the founders moved locations, rented an upper floor in a non-descript small office building. They called it simply the June 4th Museum. "Tiananmen" was not a story nervous Hong Kong officials wanted to be told, especially not to visiting mainland tourists who flocked to Hong Kong to shop. The museum's three rooms displayed a dented motorcycle helmet, a worn T-shirt, crumpled posters and blurry videos. By 2021, even their unprovocative name and obscure location proved too exposed. Volunteers packed up the artifacts and closed the museum.

In Sarajevo, one can visit a pocket-sized museum providing a minute-by-minute account of how Serbian nationalist militiamen murdered 7,000 Bosnian Muslim men and boys at Srebrenica in 1995 and, importantly, how international peacekeeping troops (Dutch soldiers) failed to prevent the massacre. The questions that the small museum's curators leave hanging still hover over post-war Bosnia and over the Netherlands and the United Nations.[162]

The Manzanar National Historic Park challenges post-war triumphalism. Authorized by the US Congress in 1992, the park is part of a partial restoration package, acknowledging the unfairness of the US government's detention of 120,000 Japanese Americans during World War II. Manzanar, located in the California desert, was one of several detention camps built by federal authorities to imprison-without-trial Japanese American women and men. Visitors today can learn a wartime history – told by Japanese Americans themselves – that might make them more curious about how militarization fuels and justifies racism.[163]

A handful of post-war museum projects are explicitly dedicated to making visible women's earlier wartime experiences. After years of collecting racially diverse women's recorded memoirs, artifacts and historical research, the Rosie the Riveter Museum opened as an official National Park Service site in 2000, in the industrial port city of Richmond, California. The World War II story it tells is not only of women obtaining well-paying industrial wartime jobs, but of their being pushed out of those jobs when "the boys came home."[164]

Then there is Tokyo's Women's Active Museum on War and Peace.[165] Its feminist staff members also chose an upper floor of a small, out-of-the-way office building for their museum. Getting there takes stamina and familiarity with the city's sprawling subway system. There is no museum sign at the building's ground-floor entrance. Most visible to casual passersby is a wedding shop. A museum visitor has to know to walk upstairs to the museum's door.

Upon entering, a visitor is immediately faced with photographic portraits of dozens of women. Each woman had been a so-called "comfort woman."

Six decades after Japan's World War II loss, the "comfort women issue" remains salient in Japanese politics. Japanese nationalists today fiercely object to efforts to document and apologize for the Japanese Imperial Army's 1930s–40s systematic enslavement of women to serve in its Asia-wide military brothel system. That is why the feminists who founded and staff this small museum do what they can to assure its safety. Post-war feminist museums are contested spaces.

As conceived by Japanese feminist journalist and human-rights campaigner the late Yayori Matsui, the Women's Active Museum has a double post-war mission. First, it is intended to teach post-war Japanese generations about the realities of World War II, including the imperial government's systematic sexual abuse of Asian women. Equipped with that knowledge, the museum's supporters hope, citizens will resist nationalists' post-war efforts to whitewash Japanese imperialism and remilitarize Japan. Second, Matsui and her successors seek to weave new bonds of feminist solidarity between Japanese feminists and anti-militarist feminists throughout Asia. That solidarity, however, depends on building mutual trust. Trust, in turn, is built on honesty. Consequently, Japanese feminists must publicly acknowledge what their government did in their name to women in Korea, China, Taiwan, the Philippines, Singapore, Cambodia, Thailand, Indonesia, Myanmar and Papua New Guinea.

One display is a large regional map of Asia. It is the product of decades of post-war collaborative research by Asian feminists. Dozens of bright red dots mark the "comfort stations" that the imperial military established – from then-northern Korea to then-Burma. It is a feminist-informed map provoking feminist post-war reflection.

A corollary embraced by the museum's curators is that those women who survived the sexual slavery that masqueraded as the "comfort women" system deserve utmost respect. Their speaking out about their wartime enslavement was not simply to become fodder for Japanese feminist atonement. Instead, women survivors who have told the museum staff their stories, or who have given permission for their photographs to be displayed at the Tokyo museum, did so on their own terms. Two full walls display women survivors' photographs. Each looks directly at the viewer. No two women are identical.

The Women's Active Museum is one of the groups selected to be named on the ICC's Gender Justice Legacy Wall.

∽

The drive from Bogotá's new airport to the capital's downtown took about forty-five minutes. Colombia's war still raged. Colombian feminists were still organizing to have a voice in the peace negotiations between the men of the government and the men of the largest insurgent force, the FARC. Already, though, international investors were anticipating peace. The evidence: towers of shiny glass skyscrapers lining the airport-to-downtown highway.

Investors and bankers. Mining executives and construction contractors. Grain traders and property developers. These are key players in any post-war society. They comprise a masculinized network of people who seek to profit from post-war reconstruction.

These profit-seeking reconstruction players, the international agency officials (from the International Monetary Fund, the European Union, the US Treasury) and the country's post-war ministries who work with them at a local level (Finance, Housing, Commerce, Public Works, Mining, Agriculture) do not think to do gender analysis. Local officials worry about the ruined economy, tax revenue reduced to a trickle, demobilized soldiers returning to a decimated job market. They look out at the rubble, the scorched farms. They are desperate to rebuild. They meet with the foreign investors and their bankers, who impose their terms. They make their plans, sign their agreements. They approach post-war reconstruction as if spreadsheets, shareholders, debt repayments and profit margins explain and justify every post-war reconstruction decision.[166]

Social services. They can come later. Reweaving the social safety net. Later. Women's full-time employment. Later. Reparations. Later. Investigating corruption. Later.

Rarely, if ever, are transnational or local feminists invited to sit at the reconstruction deal-making tables, in Brussels, Berlin or Washington. The ground-level knowledge of the complex realities of women's lives is routinely excluded from these crucial reconstructimon calculations and commitments.

This doesn't mean that women's advocates don't think about post-war reconstruction. They do. Feminist economists, feminist social workers, feminist public-health specialists, feminist agricultural specialists, feminist environmental researchers have accumulated gritty understandings of what an effective post-war reconstruction plan *should* include.[167]

First, such a reconstruction plan should guarantee that post-war governments have the funds and personnel to provide effective public education, pensions and health care, including accessible reproductive care. That is, gender-smart post-war reconstruction planners would not presume, as so many finance professionals do, that providing public services and a social safety net are mere burdens, burdens that a country in ruins cannot afford, burdens that should be shrunk.

Second, a feminist-informed post-war reconstruction plan would include the commitments necessary to assure that women had access to decently paid jobs in both the urban and rural sectors. That is, women would not be relegated to sewing and cooking classes, and would not be presumed to be the chief providers of the unpaid care for children and the war-wounded required by a post-war society.

Third, a gender-smart post-war reconstruction plan would treat environmental sustainability as necessary for the long-term security of both women and men. That is, it would not presume that short-term profitability – from agribusiness, banking, construction and mining – was a priority, regardless of its environmental risks.

A reconstruction process that would produce such a national plan would require gender impact studies of every proposed investment: every highway, every housing development, every energy project, every port expansion, every mine. The findings of each gender impact study would have to be made public and taken seriously by policy-makers and investors. There would be authoritative mechanisms for investigating corruption and holding planners, contractors and investors accountable.

The most recent in-depth gender-conscious report on the effects of a peace agreement is an investigation of the 1995 Dayton Peace Agreement, which ended the four-year war in the former Yugoslavia. The report's authors reflect on the twenty-five years of Bosnian post-war reality. The ambitious study was conducted by two Bosnian feminist researchers, Nela Porobić and Gorana Mlinarević. They titled their report *The Peace That is Not*.[168]

The Peace That is Not serves as a warning. It is a warning-in-neon to women in any society blighted by armed conflict and yearning for peace: watch out for the men who plan post-war reconstruction; their interests will not be women's interests; their interests, if allowed to be prioritized, will distort women's lives for years to come.

Porobić and Mlinarević reveal in sharp detail what happens – economically, politically and culturally – to women and men in a post-war society when the peace negotiators not only are men, but are men who have no gender analytical skills, no feminist curiosity and no co-operative interactions with feminist civil-society activists – and who arrogantly act as though they don't need any.

Among the devastating findings of *The Peace That is Not* is that the Dayton Peace Agreement negotiators – both the international men and the local male elites – cared little about ordinary Bosnians. Like past colonizers, they carved up post-war Bosnia and Herzegovina in a way that reinforced past ethnocentrism and the power of male ethno-nationalist elites. As if that were not disastrous enough, the international negotiators meeting in Dayton, Ohio, far from any Bosnian civil-society activists, marginalized the United Nations and gave authority to govern post-war Bosnian society to NATO, the world's most powerful military alliance.

Male soldiers poured into the war-torn country. Sex trafficking boomed. International police officers and soldiers were among the traffickers and customers. Officials turned a blind eye. One dismissed the trafficked women as mere "whores of war." Most of the girls and women trafficked into post-war Bosnia were from Moldova and Ukraine.[169]

Porobić and Mlinarević conclude:

The exclusion of women was obviously not a result of women being silent, inactive, or for the lack of their demands for inclusion. It was the male elites in power that did not see women as relevant actors in dealing with 'male matters of war.'[170]

TEN

Militarization Starts during Peacetime

AMONG WILDLIFE CONSERVATIONISTS THERE is a growing consensus that rural women's knowledge of local environments is crucial for building ecosystems that can sustain both humans and wild animals. With that consensus have come determined local and transnational efforts to recruit more women into national ranger workforces. Rangering has traditionally been a masculinized occupation, fueled by assumptions that rangers must be brave, able to live in rough conditions, rely on brotherly mutual support and able to spend weeks away from their homes and families. Today, at a time when those masculinizing recruitment presumptions are being challenged, a counter trend is perpetuating the masculinization of ranger forces, from Zambia to Vietnam: militarization.

Illegal poaching – of rhino horns, elephant tusks, wild songbirds – is a threat to wildlife. Rangers are mandated to prevent poaching. In recent years, male poachers – with the aid of their acquisitive criminal clients – have equipped themselves with heavy weapons. Ranger forces have responded in kind. As gender specialist Joni Seager observes, "It's an arms race."[171]

Seager has tracked the gender dynamics and consequences of that arms race. The heavier the weaponry rangers carry, the more likely it is that masculinity will be seen by recruiters as necessary for effective rangering. That, in turn, narrows the gateway for women to enter ranger forces. The result of that sexist narrowing is a loss of the essential knowledge and skills that women can bring into rangering. Women are excluded; conservation suffers.

Seager also found that the militarizing effects of the wildlife conservation arms race are rippling out beyond the workforce. Male rangers who are issued guns bring those guns home, as do the now more heavily armed poachers. Guns proliferate in rural communities where previously there were no or few guns. Men in possession of guns, even if they don't fire them, intensify masculinized intimidation of women within families.[172]

Militarization is a sneaky process that intertwines ideas, relationships and practices. It creeps, it seeps, it lures. That is, militarization doesn't usually enter with a bang or a burst of trumpets. It progresses slowly, over time. Militarization may have many proponents, some with deep pockets, but it is rarely a coherent, centralized project. Because so much of militarization happens inside our minds, it is hard to track.

Militarization is a step-by-step process that transforms individuals, institutions and communities. It is fueled by ideas. A teenage girl can be militarized if she begins to imagine a man in military uniform as an attractive mate. So can a professional sport, if its executives begin using battlefield metaphors to make games more exciting to sponsors and fans. An advertising agency can be militarized if its business strategies depend on attracting defense contractors as clients. So can a marriage, if that relationship begins to rely on the civilian wife absorbing the labor expectations imposed by her soldier-husband's employer. Professors can be militarized if they accept defense ministry research funding in exchange for keeping their findings out of the public domain. An LGBTQ movement can be militarized if its activists hold up gay, lesbian and queer soldiers as model citizens. A legislative committee can be militarized if its civilian members internalize the world view of the military commanders they are supposed to be scrutinizing.

Ideas matter. Anything can become partially or fully militarized to the extent that it is based on admiration or assumptions of military values, money, protection, imagery, equipment, patronage or mindsets. In today's highly militarized societies – the US, Myanmar, Egypt, Syria, Israel, Yemen, Russia, Brazil, Peru, Pakistan, South Korea – many areas of life are militarized. In notably *un*-militarized societies – Iceland, Samoa, Costa Rica – those same areas (schools, marriage, policing, sports, identity, business, journalism, toys) operate quite differently.[173] Militarization can do its transformative work without much galvanized attention. Town councilors agree to erect a new war memorial in a local park. A publisher urges its authors to rewrite a popular school textbook so it skips over a wartime atrocity. A new physics PhD imagines working in a weapons lab to be exciting. Producers launch a new web-streamed drama series glorifying a past military victory. Investors raise capital for a start-up's cyber weapon. Fashion brand designers create a new "camo" line to appeal to teenagers.

Most of these changes in values, desires and beliefs occur in peacetime. Most of the people who are militarized are civilians: mothers, fathers, girls, boys, editors, film buffs, teachers, budget officers, business school professors, software engineers, mechanics, scientists, electoral candidates, voters, factory workers, athletic coaches, bankers, shareholders, church goers . . .

This is *not* to say that "militarization is all in your head." Rather, it is to underscore how dependent any militarizing transformation is on spreading certain ideas – about security, success, loyalty, belonging, caring, excitement. Those ideas shape practices and relationships. Resisting those ideas is a form of anti-militarism activism.

Feminists have revealed how and why this militarizing process depends on patriarchal ideas about both men and women. That is, militarizing processes may feature and privilege certain ideas about specific sorts of manliness – the war hero, the weapons scientist, the commander-turned-politician – but they require women's complicity to move forward. Militarism therefore wraps itself in the camouflage of maternalism, wifely loyalty, feminized gratitude, even women's equality.

To fully understand militarization, feminists have learned, we need to shine a bright light on how girls and women become militarized. Judging those militarized girls and women is not enough; we need to be *interested* in them. We need to stay curious about the lives of women as wives, mothers, widows and girlfriends; curious about women as careerists, patriots, civil servants, voters, volunteers and rape survivors. Militarism's promoters try to turn each into fodder for militarization. The promoters don't necessarily succeed. Yet feminist researchers pay attention when they do. Their studies of women – in Germany, Italy, France, Britain – who were attracted to fascism and its militarized beliefs during the 1920s–30s are instructive today.[174] Likewise, profiles of those Chilean women who rallied around Pinochet's military overthrow of the leftist Allende government in the 1980s remain valuable.[175]

As feminists reveal how militarization depends not only on ideas about and held by men, but also on ideas about and held by women, women gain leverage. That is, if militarization can be stalled or reversed by women rejecting certain beliefs or resisting certain expectations, women are empowered and militarization is slowed. If a war widow refuses to be made a model of wartime sacrifice, she restrains militarizing processes. If a wife urges her soldier-husband not to re-enlist, she throws gravel on the militarizing path. If an ambitious woman member of a male-dominated legislature refuses to stay quiet about an excessive defense budget in order to advance her career, she complicates militarization. If a teenage girl tells her friends that wearing camo isn't hip, she stymies militarization. When a rape survivor refuses to become a symbol for collective revenge, militarizers are frustrated.

Militarism is not one idea. It's a package of ideas – distinct, often contradictory, ideas. Many of those ideas are gendered, depending on assumptions about femininity and masculinity. The process by which any militarized idea is promoted is gendered, reliant on the assumption that men more than women are naturally more rational, less guided by emotions. Whether at the dinner table or in public debate, rational men, it is widely imagined, will teach naive women about the militarized ways of the world.[176]

"The world is a dangerous place."

"Men are the natural protectors of women and children."

"Women are grateful for men's protection."

"The nation must be protected against those who don't belong."

"Soldiers are first-class citizens."

"Nuclear weapons are best left to experts."

"The fog of war makes accountability impossible."

That's not the entire militarized package. More ideas are wrapped into it. The package can't be swallowed all at once in a big gulp. A person may initially adopt just one militarized belief when it matches their own interpretation of a personal experience – loss, achievement or fright:

"It's natural to have enemies."

"The world is divided into 'us' and 'them.'"

"Hierarchy enhances organizational effectiveness."

"Soldiering turns a boy into a man."

"Wartime defeat is a national humiliation."

"War is the most serious public topic."

"Ethnic hatreds are ancient, rooted too deeply to be reversed."

The militarism package is expansive. The wealth of ideas that are stuffed into its wrappings make it seductive. Moreover, most militarized ideas don't seem hateful, aggressive or warmongering. Each militarized idea is portrayed as simply describing the way the world is or should be:

"War stories are exciting."

"The best guarantor of a nation's security is a strong military."

"Boys will be boys."

"Militaries teach discipline."

"Peace movements are naive."

"War is best left to men."

There are still more:

"In the end, violence is the only solution."

"A woman whose son joins the military is a proud mother."

"Patriots support the country's military."

"Guns make us safer."

"War is part of the human condition."[177]

For each of these ideas, however, there is an alternative: the world is a co-operative place. Childcare is a serious public issue. Guns make us vulnerable. Soldiering damages many men. Past military defeats teach us the value of peace. Patriots work at battered women's shelters.

Because there are alternatives, militarized ideas need to be normalized. Each idea needs to be *made* to seem as though it is the only thing a reasonable person would believe. To everyone else: "What planet are you living on?" "Are you really that naive?' Naivete is deeply feminized in most cultures. A man who is ridiculed by other men for his alleged naivete is being tarred with the brush of femininity. In a patriarchal society, most men work hard not to be feminized. A feminized man, it is patriarchally imagined, is a man who lacks the character to be trusted with public authority.

Naivete and rationality are typically treated as opposites. A naive person, it is claimed, refuses to face uncomfortable realities. A rational person looks at reality without blinking. In many cultures "rationality" is masculinized. That is, it is seen to be a natural accompaniment of trustworthy manliness. When feminists challenge militarized ideas, they necessarily question commonly supposed naivete and conventional criteria for rationality.

∽

The Jewish/Palestinian feminist campaign Gun Free Kitchen Tables (GFKT) challenges militarized ideas with data, carefully collected data. GFKT's activist researchers showed that women were being killed by male partners working as private security who brought their guns home from work. They joined with Palestinian women to debunk the popular notion that guns make women safer.[178]

Christine Ahn and her Women Cross DMZ activists have challenged militarized thinking with their feet. In 2015, they walked from North Korea to South Korea. Among the walkers were Nobel laureates Leymah Gbowee and Mairead Maguire, but central to their strategy has been engaging women from both North Korea and South Korea. By walking across the "Demilitarized Zone" that divides Koreans, these feminists have challenged a wartime mentality that normalizes the presumption of war-without-end.[179]

ICAN – the International Campaign to Abolish Nuclear Weapons – challenges supposed expertise. ICAN won the Nobel Peace Prize in 2017 for persuading sixty-eight governments to ratify the Treaty to Prohibit Nuclear Weapons. They convinced diplomats that banning nuclear weapons was not a naive goal and was not an issue best left to nuclear experts. Instead, it was a humanitarian issue. The knowledge ICAN campaigners featured was that of Australian and Pacific Indigenous women who had lived under nuclear weapons testing.[180]

At busy city intersections women come dressed in black. With silence, these feminists disrupt the flows of cars and shoppers in wartime and militarized peacetime. They call themselves Women in Black. Without funders, membership lists or formal resolutions, Women in Black groups in Osaka, Tokyo, Belgrade, Madrid, New York, Haifa and Jerusalem have challenged the militarizing notions that the nation is exclusivist and that violence solves anything. London's Women in Black hold their weekly vigil at the foot of the towering statue of the World War I nurse, Edith Cavell. Chiseled into its base is a quote from Cavell: "Patriotism is not enough. I must have no hatred or bitterness for anyone."[181]

∽

Even in a patriarchal society, militarization can be piecemeal, less than full-blown. An individual may hold one or two militarized beliefs, yet resist adopting them all. For instance, under dire conditions, even an anti-violence feminist activist may decide that a militarized defensive response to aggression is necessary. Yet that same feminist will strongly resist the argument that "boys will be boys" and will flatly reject the belief that the "fog of war" makes accountability impossible. Similarly, a woman who may be grateful for her veteran-husband's military pension will advise her son to leave the country rather than be conscripted into what she assesses to be an unnecessary war.

Militarization can seem a slippery slope: adopting several of these beliefs makes it easier to imagine the reasonableness of the others. But militarization is not an all-or-nothing proposition. It can be partial. It may progress and then be stopped in its tracks.

When material conditions start to contravene people's established ideas, militarization can be reversed. This has happened in the case of civilians' acceptance of military bases in their midst. For instance, civilians who have lived in a military base town for generations – in North Carolina, Texas, Puerto Rico, South Korea, Heidelberg, Red Deer, Canada – have grown up being told that the nearby military base has enhanced their own personal economic security. Later, when environmentalists reveal that the base has been secretly polluting the community's ground water with its uncontrolled oil run-off, those same civilians may start to question what constitutes local security.

Or a military base's local operations – job opportunities, shops' clientele, holiday parties, dating, political influence – have long appeared integral to local civilians' very sense of themselves. Their collective pride, well-being and place in the world may seem to depend on hosting a military base. Then the base closes (usually without the agreement of local civilians), and civilians gradually discover that they can create new opportunities and new identities. They no longer feel reliant on the military. They become less militarized.

Often it has been women who have led campaigns to change people's minds about the benefits of hosting a military base. It is not that being female automatically makes a woman anti-militarist. It is that women often see the justifications for hosting a military base as having so little to do with what makes their lives feel genuinely secure. Three of the best-known anti-bases campaigns led by women have opposed US military bases in Okinawa, Japan, Subic Bay, the Philippines and Greenham Common, England.[182]

In each, ideas about gender played crucial roles in mobilizing the anti-base protests. Women campaigners argued that military men endangered the safety of local girls and women, that military men colluded with local men to promote prostitution, and that national security elites were deeply mistaken in imagining that nuclear weapons protected women. Today, there are negotiations between American and Philippine officials to re-establish US military bases in the Philippines, in the name of protecting Taiwan from Chinese aggression. Where will Filipina activists be?[183]

After World War II, Icelanders were pressured by the US into joining NATO, but they refused to create their own military. Costa

Ricans once had a national military, but in 1948 decided that having a state armed force only jeopardized their security, and so they eliminated their military. During the Reagan administration, when the US government waged wars in Central America, Costa Ricans rejected efforts by Americans to slyly convert their police force into a military.

Germans' ideas about how best to reconstruct their defeated society promoted demilitarization. The process was not merely imposed on them by the war's victors. Rather, Germans living in West Germany decided, in the wake of World War II, that their future collective security lay not in building a large military force, but in joining with their former adversaries, the Dutch, Belgians and the French, to create a post-war European economic community. They were pressured to join NATO and to host both British and American military bases, but they eschewed projecting their own military's influence internationally.

Many Japanese similarly embraced demilitarization as a strategy for reconstruction in the aftermath of World War II. Again, it is patronizing to imagine that the post-war constitution was simply foisted on Japan's unwilling civilians. Instead, many Japanese became personally invested in that formative document, especially in its famous Article 9, which prohibited the Japanese government from creating a military force capable of, or deployed for, aggressive purposes. One consequence is that the Japanese military – the Japanese Self-Defense Forces – is not where Japanese young men today think they can prove their manly adulthood. Better, most young men think, try for a corporate post. In addition, Japanese young men are lowering the birth rate by marrying later and having children later, or not at all. The SDF is currently having trouble attracting male recruits.[184] Japanese women, besides not giving birth to the next generation of soldiers, have been in the majority when demonstrators have gathered outside the Diet, the national legislature, to protest the conservative government's attempts to weaken Article 9.

In the present era of Russian military aggression in Ukraine and the Chinese regime's military expansion, there is a tendency among national security experts to ridicule the post-World War II demilita-rizing cultures adopted by Germany and Japan. Condescension is abroad as militarized commentators watch both Japanese and Germans reluctantly remilitarize. As if, "Finally, Germans and Japanese are growing up, shedding their naivete." This militarized condescension by so many experts is accompanied by a strong whiff of patriarchy. The allegedly rational militarizing men are smugly chastising those allegedly feminized men who have resisted flexing their military muscles.

Japanese and German feminists may be alarmed at both Vladimir Putin's and Xi Jinping's militarizing agendas without unthinkingly jumping on board the re-militarization bandwagon. Critiquing the former does not mean embracing the latter. Japanese feminists remain committed to Article 9. German feminists still value the EU over NATO. Neither treat the concept of feminist foreign policy as a joke. They build solidarity with Ukrainian feminists. They keep their eyes on patriarchy.

∽

While militarizers like to portray it as inevitable, militarization is not an unstoppable engine. The fact that it rests on so many different beliefs and values and that it needs so many different sorts of women and men to internalize those ideas makes militari-zation vulnerable. Not only political commentators, but historians, sociologists and psychologists can pick apart militarism, idea by idea; so can artists, street performers and novelists; so can econo-mists and anthropologists.[185]

Moreover, because, to be sustainable, militarization must infect many different social sectors, critics of militarization can employ a wide range of skills and talents to challenge it: art, theater, storytelling, campaigning, librarianship, parenting, reporting, legislating, forensics. Feminist critics of militarization are using them all.[186]

In 1910, before the First World War was even imagined, Virginia Woolf and a group of her brother's friends staged an irreverent, somewhat lighthearted hoax at Weymouth, the Royal Navy's port.

Dressed up fancifully as Abyssinian royalty, they managed to board Britain's then most formidable warship, the *Dreadnought*. Pulling off the hoax made the Royal Navy look foolish. Making a military look foolish is an anti-militarizing move. It was more than a decade later, nevertheless, as the Great War's losses became appallingly clear, that Virginia Woolf directed her writing energies to explicitly bursting the balloon of militarism.

In 1928, Woolf gave lectures at two of Cambridge University's women's colleges, Newnham and Girton. Together, her lectures became *A Room of One's Own*. While the patriarchal barriers facing women writers was her chief theme, Woolf made clear how militarization entrenched those barriers. Yes, she told the young women sitting there in front of her – women who were too young to remember much of the Great War – in the past, patriarchy had given upper-class British men access to universities that women could then only dream of entering, but the kind of education those men acquired imbued them with desires and values that would ruin their lives and the lives of whole societies. That militarized, masculinized elite civilian education would nurture in them:

... the instinct for possession, the rage for acquisition, which drives them to desire other people's fields and goods perpetually; to make frontiers and flags; battleships and poison gas; to offer up their own lives and their children's lives.[187]

Virginia Woolf continued to think about the deadly interplay of militarism, masculinity and patriarchy, and the ways they normalized each other and lured so many women into complicity. That thinking culminated in Woolf's remarkable 1938 book *Three Guineas*. In her diaries and letters, Woolf predicted that even her closest Bloomsbury male friends would detest this book. She was right. They protested Woolf's holding even seemingly well-meaning upper-middle-class men – professors, lawyers, writers, clerics, barristers, senior civil servants – responsible for perpetuating the patriarchal practices and the ideas that made the looming next world war inevitable.[188] *Three Guineas* is as powerful today as it was on the eve of the last world war.

Feminists have been spelling out the alternatives to militarizing ideas since at least 1900. They published in newspapers and magazines. They gave lectures to local groups. They made speeches at women's conferences. To prevent war, they called for the end of imperialism, reduction of armaments, creation of transnational co-operative institutions, an end to racism, and women's participation in policy making. Irish thinker Dorothy Macardle, Jamaican British thinker Una Marson, Austrian thinker Bertha von Suttner, British thinkers Lucie A Zimmern, Vera Brittain and Elizabeth Wiskemann, US thinkers Jane Addams and Emily Greene Balch, French thinker Simone Weil, African American thinkers Anna Julia Cooper and Mary Church Terrell: today, nonetheless, the ideas of these women are scarcely mentioned in the current "canon" of influential theories of international politics.

But that is changing. And, with that change, the long history of women's challenges to militarized thinking is becoming more visible. Women's anti-militarist thinking is starting to look less idiosyncratic, less naive . . . more rational.[189]

∽

Across generations, we have learned that militarized ideas, even when challenged and temporarily consigned to the proverbial dustbin, however, can re-emerge. The cloak of masculinized rationality can be washed, ironed and draped anew over those old ideas. Once-debunked ideas can resurface to re-energize old believers and gain new adherents.

Still, militarization is not inevitable. It is not unstoppable. It is not all or nothing. It depends on people holding certain ideas, telling certain patriarchal stories that support certain patriarchal lessons. Those ideas can be challenged. Those stories can be rewritten. Those war-inspiring lessons can be *un*learned.

Taking women's and girls' pre-war, wartime and post-war lives seriously is crucial for demilitarizing a society. Women who take action – with data, their feet, their redefinition of expertise, their silent disruptions of traffic – can expose narrow ideas, broaden people's understandings, roll back re-emerging militarization.

Together, we are learning to stay alert, to remain creatively active. By sharing our experiences, trading our strategies, recording our findings, the reinflated balloon of militarized thinking can be punctured again. There is always work for the newest generation of feminists to do.

ELEVEN

Ukrainian Feminists Have Lessons to Teach Us about War

OLGA PLAKHOTNIK CAME TO Odesa to meet with other Ukrainian feminist activists. It was a small gathering, hosted by two transnational feminist groups. We all sat in a circle in an airy room on the ground floor of the Hotel Londonskaya. Though faded, the hotel, fronting onto Odesa's famous tree-lined promenade, seemed a bit grand for a gathering of grassroots activists. In its heyday, the Londonskaya had been a destination for such notables as Anton Chekhov and Isadora Duncan. Plaques outside upstairs bedrooms marked where they had stayed. In the hotel's interior courtyard was a tree that, according to local lore, was planted where Pushkin once sat.[190]

It was June, 2018. Four years earlier, the Russian army had seized the Ukrainian peninsula of Crimea. Simultaneously, Moscow-backed Russian nationalists had launched a separatist war in Ukraine's eastern Donbas region. Odesa wasn't yet in a war zone. People strolled along the promenade, under the shade of the trees, taking photos of each other on the Potemkin Steps, enjoying performances at the famous Odesa Opera House. But Olga and her colleagues were feminists acting and thinking in wartime. Not surprisingly, there was a low-level tension in the hotel meeting room. Could they trust each other? Was anyone there a stealth nationalist? As we went around the circle introducing ourselves, each participant described her own activist work. Everyone else leaned forward to listen between the lines. Most of the Ukrainian women were meeting each other for the first time.

Olga described her work in a co-operative group publishing a small Ukrainian journal that served as a forum for sharing and debating feminist ideas. Next to her were three women who had started a community theater group. They put on plays they hoped would engage women in their own complex lives. The next woman in the circle told of her tiny group's efforts in Donbas to help elderly Ukrainian women get to medical appointments. Most of Donbas's doctors and nurses already had fled the military violence, but a small clinic remained open. The drive to the clinic that used to take them forty-five minutes now took over two hours – navigating the proliferating armed check points that pock-marked wartime Donbas – and was now hazardous.

Feminist activism in a war zone can turn into humanitarian work. This has been the experience of feminists in Syria, Congo, Kashmir, Liberia and Northern Ireland, as well as in wartime Britain, Poland, France and the US. Historically, organizing to perform care work has been, for many women, a path both to and from explicitly women's rights work. Feminist work and humanitarian work are not in opposition. Rather, these two sorts of women's community engagement are in constant conversation. Humanitarian work cannot be dismissed as mere women's work; feminist work should not be sidelined as narrowly political work.

Some women who shy away from feminist activism because it seems "too political," "too controversial" or "too dangerous" will readily join a women-led group providing medical care, emergency housing or food distribution. Those experiences, while not overtly political, can have political consequences, honing women's skills in speaking and organizing, while revealing to them the arrogance or incompetence of male policy-makers. For politically anxious women, engaging in those humanitarian activities also can forge new bonds of trust with the activist women they had been taught to fear.

Doing humanitarian work in Donbas in 2018 wasn't the first experience of organizing humanitarian work in war zones for Ukrainian women. Ukrainian historian Martha Bohachevsky-Chomiak tells of Ukrainian women political activists joining war work organizations in both World Wars I and II. Some became nurses, others ran hospitals. Still others worked with the thousands of war-displaced persons and the children orphaned by war. During both wars, Ukrainian women organizing humanitarian care had to avoid scrutiny and interference from competing imperial forces fighting for control of Ukraine.[191]

For those women already involved in local feminist political organizing, a sudden crisis – a flood, an earthquake, a military invasion – and the immediacy of people's distress motivate them to plunge into efforts to meet urgent physical needs. In responding to emergencies, women activists may create new partnerships, often working side by side with women with whom they have never before felt comfortable, divided as women are by party, age, class, region, generation, religion or ethnicity. Doing humanitarian work doesn't mean that their feminist attentiveness or feminist goals are shunted aside. Rather, these Ukrainian grassroots feminists teach us, those feminist understandings are deepened by doing the work it takes to get an elderly rural woman through military checkpoints to a health clinic.

The three-day meeting in Odesa was full of learning, but it ended without a commitment to further joint action. Several years later, now in the midst of the full-fledged defensive war against Putin's aggression, Olga Plakhotnik reflected on the Odesa gathering: "We needed more time together to build trust among each other."[192] The agenda-attentive hosts, though supportive, hadn't realized how Ukraine's already fraught political climate was sowing mistrust and misunderstanding even among seemingly natural allies. Simply being Ukrainian women doing feminist grassroots work was not by itself enough to create the level of trust required for action-committed solidarity. Building feminist solidarity when militarism is escalating can take time, long walks and lots of coffee.

∽

Oksana Potapova was part of a five-member group commissioned by UN Women to research and write a "rapid response" report on Ukrainian women. There was a sense of urgency. They had to make visible to the international community the on-the-ground realities shaping the lives of Ukraine's diverse women. Just a month before they began their investigation, on February 24, 2022, Putin's military had launched a full-scale attack on Ukraine. Russian tanks were heading for Kyiv.

UN Women, an agency of the United Nations, didn't exist when the women of Serbia, Croatia, Kosovo and Bosnia were engulfed by ethno-nationalist armed conflict in 1992. UN Women didn't exist when Rwanda's Hutuist forces launched their rape-laced genocidal violence in 1994. It was barely getting off the ground when autocratic regimes turned security forces on their own democracy-seeking citizens in 2011's Arab Spring. It had taken an alliance of feminists inside and outside the UN to assess the patriarchal structures that were making it impossible to get the sprawling UN organization to take women's rights seriously. Having done their feminist assessment, these women then drafted a plan for the creation of UN Women, lobbying state delegates to authorize it in 2012.[193]

A decade after its launch, UN Women still was woefully under-funded, given its sprawling global mandate. UN Women staffers, nonetheless, sought to support women in Ukraine in the weeks following the February invasion. They put together a network of researchers, sponsors and funders to conduct a wartime gender-explicit investigation. Their partner was the international humanitarian aid group CARE, which included its own gender-conscious staffers. UN Women then sought and received funding from the governments of Canada and Norway, and from CARE Germany. This networking is what it took for UN Women to hire five feminist researchers, including Oksana Potapova, to create the *Rapid Gender Analysis of Ukraine* in month two of the war.[194]

Potapova and her co-researchers decided to use a combination of qualitative and quantitative investigatory methods. They realized that, while reliable statistics matter, by themselves data could not adequately demonstrate the special wartime challenges facing Ukrainian women. Oksana's own research strategies were shaped by both her academic training and her prior experience in feminist theater production. Working with Ukraine's Theatre for Dialogue, she had introduced ideas such as peacebuilding, gender equality and sexual harassment in settings that enabled women to work out their own experiences of each. Personal storytelling and body work, for instance, encouraged women displaced by the Donbas conflict to express their emotions and perceptions. By 2019, theater-based feminist activism had taught her that seeing Ukrainians simplistically as men and women didn't capture the particular realities that policies needed to address. For instance:

> Single mothers face very specific challenges in Ukraine; displaced face specific challenges. We are still living in a men's world, where men are supposed to work outside and bring back a living wage, while childcare is left over to women . . .
>
> When you're displaced . . . you're cut off from your network, you're left hustling alone without anybody to help . . .[195]

The gender picture in Ukraine just prior to the February 24, 2022 invasion shaped how women and men coped with that militarized aggression when it exploded in their lives. Women's relationships to both men and the state were not what they were when Ukrainians endured the violence of world war. Over seventy-five years, Ukrainian women's literacy – long a goal of Ukrainian women activists – had expanded to the point that women's literacy now equaled men's, each over 90%. Literacy is a crucial tool in coping with war. As feminists had learned in other war zones, a woman who has not had the chance to learn how to read and write (and count) is a woman made more dependent on literate men in wartime.

Furthermore, by the early twenty-first century, more Ukrainian women were going to university and joining Ukraine's formal workforce. Nonetheless, going into the current war, Ukrainian women were far from equal to Ukrainian men. For instance, only five of the government's twenty-four cabinet members were women. As one woman Member of Parliament told a journalist, "There is definitely more masculine decision-making at the top level, meaning women's voices are not decisive."[196]

Gender inequality, Potapova and her fellow researchers argued, would significantly affect how women coped with, and made, policies to address the current war's violence and displacement.

Paid work. A woman without paid work is far less likely to be able to cope with war. She has less money of her own. She therefore has to depend economically on a husband, son or father – if they are present and willing to share. That, in turn, means she has less autonomy to make her own wartime strategic calculations and to act on them. In 2020, on the eve of the Russian invasion, only 51% of Ukrainian adult women had jobs that paid. By contrast, 62% of Ukrainian adult men were in paid work. All Ukrainian women worked, of course, but most of women's daily work – childcare, finding and cooking food, caring for the ill, doing family farm work, caring for elderly family members – was *un*paid. Of all Ukrainian adult women, 49% went into the current war without income of their own.

As feminists around the world know, women securing paid work is not the end of the gendered economic story. Oksana Potapova and her UN Women colleagues paid attention to what sorts of jobs with what levels of pay those employed Ukrainian women held. By 2021, there were Ukrainian women working as museum curators, school-teachers, software engineers, university professors, nurses, scientists, civil servants and television scriptwriters. But other Ukrainian women in the country's paid labor force were working as low-waged garment factory sewers, domestic workers, sex workers, office cleaners and restaurant workers. The UN Women researchers thus looked at the full range of paid work that Ukrainian women performed. They found that in pre-war Ukraine there was a gender pay gap of 23%. That is, on average, a Ukrainian woman holding a paid job earned the equivalent of only seventy-seven cents for every dollar that a Ukrainian man earned. Moreover, the jobs that Ukrainian women held were more likely to be precarious than the jobs men held, subject to exploitation and layoffs.[197]

When Russia launched its invasion, that gendered precarity already had been exacerbated by the 2020–21 Covid-19 global pandemic. It was women who were more likely than men to be laid off during the pandemic and it had been women more than men who had felt the need to stay home to take care of sick relatives or to help their children stay focused on online schoolwork.

There is nothing automatic in any country about women's participation in paid work steadily increasing. A health crisis or a war can throw the gendered economic gears into reverse.

In addition, the Ukrainian researchers found, more than half of all Ukrainian pre-war households were found to be headed by women. At first glance, "women-headed households" might sound like women's empowerment. It is not. It is a measure of poverty. As in virtually every country in the world, a household in Ukraine without an adult male income earner is more likely to be impoverished because women have less access to decently paid jobs, and women raising children on their own have to trim their paid work chances to fit their unpaid childcare responsibilities.

As in every society, one has to be intersectionally curious about gendered inequalities. In Ukraine, Potapova and her co-researchers found, it is Roma women who are on the bottom rung of the country's economic ethnicized, gendered ladder. Roma women are less likely than Roma men, and less likely than other Ukrainian women, to have access to paid work. When they do gain access, their work is likely to be lower paid, more likely to be in the informal sector and thus, more precarious. Roma women, already politically and socially marginalized, have confronted the challenges of war in Ukraine with few resources.[198]

Ukraine went into the current war with Europe's highest proportion of elderly women. People trying to keep track of Ukrainians' experiences of the current war may have been struck by how prevalent older women have been in news reports, in photographs of food lines, in interviews with bombing survivors. In a crisis, elderly women are commonly portrayed as mere victims. But, in reality – and in Ukraine's wartime reality – elderly women make choices: to stay or leave a frontline town, to abandon their farms or continue to plant and harvest, to take pets or leave them behind, to go underground into hiding or openly defy occupying Russian soldiers, to stay silent about war crimes they have witnessed or to volunteer evidence.

A seventy-year-old Ukrainian woman in wartime may even take on added responsibilities, becoming the chief caretaker of a grandchild when parents have gone off to fight, have traveled abroad for work or have been injured or killed. This is what Iryna Skalietska did when she fled bomb-ruined Kharkiv with her granddaughter, twelve-year-old Yeva. Iryna protected – and kept fed and energized – her granddaughter from train to train, city to city, country to country, shelter to shelter. Yeva records her wartime displacement and flight with her grandmother in her girlhood diary.[199]

Thus, the gendered politics of pensions matter. Ukraine's pre-war gender pension gap was wider than even its pay gap: 32%. That is, in 2020, on the eve of Russia's invasion, Ukrainian older women received thirty-two cents less per pension dollar than did older Ukrainian men.[200]

In wartime, governments strain to meet budgetary commitments for social safety-net services. Military expenditures push everything else aside. Those citizens most reliant on social safety-net programs before the war – kindergartens, public clinics, social workers, transportation subsidies, social housing – will be those who, once wartime mobilization takes precedence, feel the loss most profoundly. Oksana Potapova and her co-researchers revealed that as Ukraine's funded public services were cut in wartime, volunteers tried to fill the void. Most volunteer work was unpaid. Women were not only most dependent on publicly funded social services, they also became a large proportion of those who volunteered to fill in for those vanishing services. Women's humanitarian work as unpaid volunteers expanded their pre-existing unpaid care work.

An older woman told Potapova's team: "A person's activities motivate – you want to be useful. The whole family and I went to the volunteer kitchen to make dumplings on the front line. It helps you feel alive and useful today."

A woman with an infant of her own explained: "I do volunteer work to be useful to the affected people. And it distracts me from my heavy thoughts."[201]

If the Ukrainian and international (IMF, EU and US) planners for Ukraine's post-war reconstruction do not include feminist experts in their deliberations and fail to *explicitly and effectively* address the country's growing gender inequality, Ukrainian women's unequal relationships to men and the state will deepen. The peace these gender-uncurious men reconstruct for Ukraine will be a patriarchal peace.

By July 2022, in the fifth month of the full-scale war, Oksana Potapova had submitted her report to UN Women, but she herself had become one of Ukraine's millions of displaced persons. She tried to keep track of all the places where she had taken refuge. Nine so far. Nine sofas, borrowed apartments, temporary shelters. When asked by another displaced Ukrainian woman to "draw home," she used colored markers to draw a table looking out of a window onto a leafy tree. On the table she drew a small candle and a vase with fresh flowers. Potapova explained that she had crafted a little routine to make herself feel less displaced: everywhere she moved, she lit the candle and put flowers in the vase. They turned every temporary shelter into her "home."[202]

∾

Nina Potarska has co-ordinated the Ukrainian local section of transnational feminist peace organization WILPF. In the months before Putin's full-scale invasion, Nina was attentive to – alarmed by – the increasingly militarized conditions that Ukrainian women faced, especially in the wake of Putin's annexation of Crimea and armed conflict in the country's east. She had to think about how to engage Ukrainian women who were enduring separatist violence in Donbas, while simultaneously advancing global feminism's peace agenda. It was not easy to do both simultaneously.

From their beginnings in the 1880s, Ukrainian women's advocacy groups have been internationally conscious. To organize women in Ukraine, local activists have had to think carefully about rival empires on each of the country's borders: the Austro-Hungarian Empire, the Russian Czarist Empire, the German Empire. All three had imperialist agendas that included occupying and controlling Ukraine. In the mid-twentieth century, Ukrainian feminists had to strategize around Nazi and Soviet rival territorial appetites. Like Nina Potarska, her feminist foresisters never enjoyed the luxury of ignoring imperialist militarism in local women's lives; it was always hovering or under full sail.

In addition to being a feminist peace activist, Nina Potarska was a professor of sociology at the National Technical University in Kyiv. She also was a partner and a parent. All four of her roles would be upended by Russia's invasion. In the increasingly militarized years between 2014 and February 2022, Nina saw her activist work as researching, reporting and assessing women's rights. With her WILPF perspective guiding her activism, her work made clear how militarization and war waging privileged masculinity, while it simultaneously jeopardized women's rights and well-being.

In the tension-laced years leading up to the February 2022 invasion, it was not just Russia that appeared to pose a threat to Ukrainian independence and to women's authentic security. It also was NATO. To Nina Potarska, the US-led military alliance did not look like a savior. It looked like a stalking horse for Western patriarchal imperialism.

When Nina spoke out in 2021 against war and the warmongerers, she called out all the policy-makers – in Moscow, Washington, London and Brussels – who advocated weapons build-ups and masculinized military alliances as the solutions to regional conflict. In this, Nina shared other feminist peace activists' analysis. As WILPF's Ukrainian co-ordinator, Nina had taken part in conversations and information sharing with WILPF local feminist activists in Bosnia, Colombia, Nigeria, Cameroon, Sweden, Austria, Syria and Afghanistan.

Nina and her fellow WILPF country representatives had discussed UN Security Council Resolution 1325 (which WILPF activists had helped to draft). As different as their societies were, these feminist peace activists agreed: feminists have the gritty knowledge, skills and experience to create lasting peace; militarization cannot produce genuine peace; furthermore, a militarized peace can never deliver sustainable security to women.[203]

On February 24, the Russian military launched its violent full-scale invasion of Ukraine. Nina Potarska and her family were among the thousands of Ukrainians forced to flee. Her eleven-year-old daughter was just recovering from Covid. Nina's partner helped their child get close to the Polish border, traveling on foot for the final eight kilometers. He then had to turn back in accordance with the emergency decree requiring men of his age to stay in Ukraine to defend the country. It was a living nightmare, Nina recalled. By April, two months into the war, with the support of the Swedish feminist development group Kvinna till Kvinna, Nina had made it to Kraków, Poland. Though she had had to give up her university job, she was reunited with her young daughter. She had become a refugee:

> I have this feeling that I want to go back to Ukraine, but my colleagues beg me to stay outside, so I can speak with others and work with fundraising and manage humanitarian help. I understand that my work is important too, but mentally, my soul wants me to be together with them in Ukraine.[204]

In full-blown wartime, Nina, the Ukrainian feminist peace activist-parent-professor, was facing the terrible dilemma of staying committed to feminist peace principles while also supporting women assaulted by Russian military aggression. She was devoting her energies to doing whatever her colleagues asked of her:

> Sometimes they call me just to help them think – I sometimes feel like an "additional brain" outside Ukraine. I help them calculate the risks and make decisions. Sometimes it's about making very simple decisions, but when a person is under such huge stress, even that can be quite difficult . . . They need safe and quiet places without bombing, shelling, and noise.[205]

Death had become a daily occurrence. Every morning when Nina opened her mobile phone, she learned of another friend who had been killed in the war. Nonetheless, among the women whom Nina had tried to stay in touch with were Russian feminists. As a feminist,

Nina believed she knew that living amidst such violence could lure even a committed peace activist into hatred, a hatred that perpetuated war. Nina said she would not be lured into hatred.

∽

They named their August 2022 summer school "Thinking Under Bombing." Maria Mayerchyk and Olga Plakhotnik had persuaded a German foundation and the university in Greifswald, an ancient market town on the coast of the Baltic Sea, to host a two-week feminist summer school. The students would be women (and a few men), most of whom were Ukrainian refugees.[206]

"Thinking under bombing" – it had an Arendtian ring to it.[207] Maria and Olga, Ukrainian feminist academics, wanted to create a safe space where, at least for a few days, Ukrainian women could think together and learn from each other. Feminists, they knew, could not stop thinking when war turned their lives upside down. That was when it was crucial for women to think.

The surroundings were deceptively peaceful. With the reunification of Germany, this one-time East German town had seen its summer tourism rebound. An easy train ride north from Berlin, Greifswald offered small hotels, walks along the coast, boat trips on the canal and a weekend puppet theater. In the main square, there were stalls selling handicrafts, retro clothing and grilled-fish sandwiches. Around the square's edges were restaurants where tourists and locals could enjoy beer, wine and ice cream. Once occupied by Sweden, Greifswald had experienced multiple wars. It escaped World War II's destructive aerial bombing when the mayor came to an agreement with the assaulting military. If, however, while strolling around the town center, one casts one's eyes downward, one might see brass plaques installed reminding one that Greifswald had not been a safe space for everyone. Outside a small bookstore, the sidewalk brass plaque reads: "Here lived Dr. Gerhard Mamlok, born 1897, deported 1942, died September 8, 1942."

Maria and Olga organized their summer school around formal lectures and classes, yet left plenty of time for discussion and informal conversations. Among the class topics were Ukraine's gendered labor market (one graph showed that in 2020 men held 67% of all the Ukrainian government's senior civil service posts, women a mere 33%), recent Ukrainian women's protests (featuring the topless FEMEN Ukrainian protesters) and images of "home." Every morning, Ukrainian language instruction was offered, acknowledging that many Ukrainians whose first language was Russian might now want to become proficient in Ukrainian.

With days spent getting to know each other and peaceful surroundings providing a sense of security and leisure, Maria and Olga hoped that difficult questions might be explored. Why had Russian imperialism attracted less feminist attention globally than had British, French and American imperialisms? How could Ukrainian feminists critique militarism when waging a defensive war? There were no easy answers. The summer school was designed to build enough trust to openly talk about the tough questions. Each question mattered to feminists acting in wartime. Over the two weeks, fresh questions kept surfacing. Was it possible to resist militarized ideas and yet press the Americans to send more artillery? Was a national identity inherently incompatible with feminism?

"Thinking under bombing" wasn't about reaching unambiguous answers. It was about thinking together in wartime, as feminists.

∽

Challenging violence against women had been a principal commitment of Ukrainian feminists since national independence in 1991. Marta Chumalo, a psychologist, has been among the campaign's most determined activists. As part of that campaign, Marta co-founded Lviv's Women's Perspectives Center – an independent feminist organization dedicated to charting violence against Ukrainian women. It has pressed all arms of the government to take the violence seriously by holding perpetrators accountable and training civil servants and NGO activists in feminist analysis. It has held workshops to raise awareness of violence among diverse women. Contrary to local folk wisdom, they learn, "Beating is not a form of love."

Marta and her colleagues launched the Center in 1998, seven years after the collapse of the Soviet Union and Ukraine's formal independence. Marta and her Center colleagues lived through the country's 2004 "Orange Revolution," which, disappointingly, did not end the government's rampant corruption.

Corruption is always gendered. Women and men do not play identical roles in political and bureaucratic corruption. More often than not, while women can become corrupt, the relationships that grease the wheels of corruption are masculinized relationships, relationships that depend on certain understandings shared among well-placed men. Rule of law is meant to disrupt those distorted, anti-democratic relationships. Ukrainian women's advocates have been advocates for the rule of law because it makes governance fairer, more transparent and more open to civil society's input.[208] In the area of violence against women, police officers widely known to take bribes are not police officers to whom a woman suffering domestic violence by a male partner is likely to report abuse.[209]

Nine years after the Orange Revolution, Marta and her co-activists experienced a more effective popular uprising. Today it is referred to as the "Revolution of Dignity." From November 2013 through February 2014, Ukrainians of disparate backgrounds – students and their parents, Jews and Christians, LGBTQ activists and tradespeople, small town residents and city dwellers – flocked to the central plaza of Kyiv, the "Maidan," to challenge the increasingly corrupt and autocratic president who had caved in to Putin's demand that Ukraine give up its candidacy for EU membership. There in the Maidan, defying the regime's security forces' brutality, many Ukrainians felt as though, for the first time in Ukraine's history, they were creating a genuine civil society. There was a gender division of labor among the protestors, with mostly men building the barricades and mostly women supplying food and nursing, but everyone in the Maidan, it seemed, felt that, together, they were making history. It was a memorable collective moment.[210]

Marta and Women's Perspectives were part of the country's vibrant post-Maidan civil society. The Center's work was intended to ensure that women were full participants in the still-nascent bottom-up democracy. They argued that a woman threatened by domestic violence could not act as a full citizen. A woman subjected to any sort of violence who could not trust the police, public prosecutors or judges to effectively pursue her charges was being denied full citizenship. Without effectively challenging violence against women, the promise of Ukrainian democracy could not be fulfilled.

By 2021, in the middle of the Covid lockdown, Marta and the Center's activists were labeling the level of men's violence against Ukrainian women "femicide." They argued that the scale of male violence endured by women across Ukraine had reached such an extraordinary level that it qualified as murder of an entire class of persons. The Center announced, therefore, that it was establishing a new program: the National Femicide Watch. The project's staff would track murders of Ukrainian women, as well as police responses and prosecutorial and judicial actions. Its staff would also monitor what, if any, protective orders were issued by authorities against threatening potential perpetrators. National Femicide Watch would use its findings to lobby for reforms in both government policy and practice.[211]

To document the dire condition of women in Ukraine internationally – and to ensure that the government did not underplay its extent – Marta Chumalo and two attorneys from Women's Perspectives submitted a formal report to the UN Special Rapporteur on Violence Against Women and Girls. The Special Rapporteur had been launched by the UN Human Rights Council in 1994 under pressure from feminists inside and outside the UN who asserted that violence against women was neither merely a private affair nor only a national concern.

Violence against women, they contended, denied women the basic human rights that the UN was established to uphold.[212]

What happens to violence against women in war and how should feminists think about violence against women when militarized violence has engulfed the entire society? After the February 2022 Russian invasion, priorities shifted for Ukrainian government officials. There was less public money to support shelters for women victims of domestic violence. There were fewer police officers to respond to women's calls for protection. There was less "bandwidth" for civilian policy-makers to think about non-war-related violence against women.[213]

Marta and her feminist colleagues insisted that wartime did not make violence against women beside the point. Just the opposite. If Ukraine was going to effectively wage its defensive war against Russian aggression, the country's women, as well as its men, would need to be capable of acting as fully functioning citizens. Yet the conditions of war exacerbated the factors causing violence against women. Documented sexual abuse by occupying Russian soldiers had to be prosecuted, but those were not the only sorts of violence against Ukrainians that needed to be made public and challenged during this war. Since the invasion, more Ukrainian women in villages and cities were living on their own. There were fewer streetlights. There were more men on the streets. More Ukrainian men had guns.[214]

Marta, along with other Ukrainian feminists, stepped up their pressure on the government of President Volodymyr Zelensky and his party, Servant of the People, to push members of parliament (now one-fifth women) to ratify the Istanbul Convention on Preventing and Combating Violence Against Women. For six years, conservative members of the legislature, the Rada, backed by the country's conservative religious clergymen, had refused to ratify the Istanbul Convention, claiming that its concept of gender legitimized gay marriage and undermined the family. Zelensky and his party, though elected in 2019 in a fair election and promising to protect democracy and weed out corruption, had waffled, not wanting to upset the conservatives.[215] Feminists, however, kept pressing Zelensky and his allies. In June 2022, they prevailed. The Rada ratified the Istanbul Convention. For the first time, the Ukrainian government was legally committed to creating effective state mechanisms and practices to combat and prosecute men's violence against women.[216]

Nor did wartime take the topic of militarized masculinities off Ukrainian feminists' proverbial table. Four months after their parliamentary victory, Marta organized a feminist workshop. Women came to Lviv to take part, despite Russian missiles raining down on the country. The participants wanted to share their ideas about what men's militarization in wartime meant for women. In their own feminist and humanitarian work to support women, they were seeing Ukrainian men returning from combat taking out their anger or trauma on women in their households. This could not be shoved to the proverbial back burner. It had to be challenged by Ukrainian women now, during wartime.

∽

In early 2023, the Swedish government awarded three women activists its prestigious Olof Palme Prize. Named after the assassinated Swedish prime minister, himself an outspoken defender of human rights, the award is annually bestowed on persons who have made outstanding contributions to advancing human rights. Among previous awardees were Kofi Annan, Daniel Ellsberg and Congolese physician Denis Mukwege. The newest Olof Palme awardees included Eren Keskin, a Turkish lawyer who had worked to defend the rights of the country's ethnic and sexual minorities and women survivors of sexual violence. Despite having been jailed by the government, Keskin had won trials against several male Turkish military and civilian officials charged with sexual violence. The second awardee was Narges Mohammadi, a journalist, human rights defender and campaigner for Iranian women's rights. She is the co-founder of Iran's National Peace Council. Since November 2021, Mohammadi has been jailed by the regime in the notorious Evin prison.

The third woman chosen to receive the 2023 Olof Palme Prize was Marta Chumalo, the Ukrainian feminist. Among Marta Chumalo's activities that had impressed the Swedish award selectors were her two decades of activism against violence against women, her leadership in the campaign to ratify the Istanbul Convention and her support for Ukrainian women in the current defensive war against Russian aggression.

In her initial response to news of the award, Marta said:

> This is a great reason to speak at all levels about the fact that women's rights, especially in wartime, are often neglected and

violated. And for me, this award is a visual recognition of the efforts Ukrainian feminists are making now in Ukraine and abroad to help affected women and children to be safe, to reduce the devastating consequences of the war, and to attract solidarity and support for Ukraine from all over the world.[217]

TWELVE

Feminist Lessons Are for Everyone

A USEFUL LESSON IS always in motion. It's not static. It is not simply to be repeated by rote. A feminist lesson, especially, is kindling to fuel a fire of thinking. The feminist lessons here are twelve-and-counting. Each of these twelve lessons has emerged out of years of thinking, investigating, wondering, comparing, counting, debating, storytelling and sharing – and rethinking. Absorbing and acting on each feminist lesson makes us all more reliable in our understandings of war. That, in turn, makes us more valuable as citizens – of our countries and of the world.

Feminism isn't a club. It is an ever-expanding porous network of women and men thinking seriously about women's complex lives, about women's relationships to men, to governments and to each other. Feminism is about questioning, sharing, exploring the workings of inequity and injustice. Anyone can join in the committed wondering – wondering about wounds, wondering about expertise, wondering about "cannon fodder," wondering about security, wondering about sexual slavery, wondering about reconstruction, wondering about the "fog of war."

Warning: becoming and staying feminist in one's wondering takes stamina. That is what all the women activists portrayed in this book have shown us. Patriarchy – and those people who benefit from privileging certain sorts of masculinities – depends on the rest of us lacking stamina, getting burned out. Patriarchy counts on us withdrawing into shallow individualism, fantastical fundamentalism or pseudo-sophisticated cynicism.

Feminist stamina, however, doesn't have to be a personalized resource, stockpiled just in one's own private warehouse. Feminist stamina can be sustained by sharing dilemmas. We can build the trust it takes to admit our puzzles to others. That candor can generate sustainable stamina.

∽

Solidarity. It has such a positive, even virtuous ring. We often express solidarity with those digging through rubble after an earthquake, with those surviving a surging pandemic, with those standing up to an autocratic government.

Achieving authentic solidarity, though, is hard. Creating a feminist solidarity with women in war zones and women confronting militarized oppression is even more demanding.

Feminists working to prevent or end wars in so many countries need us to be in solidarity with them. They are teaching us, though, that to be in genuine solidarity calls for our sustained curiosity. We need to put ourselves in other girls' and women's shoes. It is not enough to be "sad." It is not enough even to be sympathetic. To become feminist in our efforts at solidarity, we need to learn about each other's gendered histories, each other's gendered economies, each other's gendered hopes and worries.

That takes work, feminist intellectual and emotional work. One can tell when one is striving for real solidarity with women experiencing militarized violence or military aggression because one feels the sort of fatigue that comes after a good workout, from stretching, imagining, listening and learning.

Maybe this is the thirteenth feminist lesson of war.

Notes

Chapter One: Women's Wars Are Not Men's Wars

1. data.worldbank.org, accessed October 30, 2022.

2. On Poland's conservative governing party and the social movement that propelled it to power: Agnieszka Graff and Elżbieta Korolczuk, *Anti-Gender Politics in the Populist Moment* (London: Routledge, 2021). On Ethiopia: Anu Kumar, "Why is the U.S. Preventing Legal Abortions in Ethiopia?" in *New York Times*, International Edition, October 26, 2022. Anu Kumar is the president and chief executive of Ipas, a non-profit civil society organization that works transnationally to increase access to contraception and safe abortions.

3. Joni Seager, *The Women's Atlas* (London: Myriad Editions, 2018; New York: Penguin Books, 2018). See also: Orly Maya Stern, *Women and War Economies* (forthcoming, 2023).

4. A recent photographic essay on two US factories making artillery shells, many destined for Ukraine, shows only male workers: John Ismay, "How to Forge Shells for Ukraine's Artillery" in *New York Times*, February 6, 2023. The photographers are Lyndon French and Natalie Keyssar.

5. Among the feminist-informed studies of wartime prostitution are: Philippa Levine, *Prostitution, Race and Politics: Policing Venereal Disease in the British Empire* (New York: Routledge, 2003); Katherine Moon, *Sex Among Allies: Military Prostitution in US-Korea Relations* (New York: Columbia University Press, 1997); Beth Bailey and David Farber, *The First Strange Place: The Alchemy of Race and Sex in World War II Hawaii*, (New York: Free Press, 1992); Yuki Tanaka, *Japan's Comfort Women: Sexual Slavery and Prostitution During World War II and the US Occupation* (New York: Routledge, 2001); Cynthia Enloe, *Maneuvers: The International Politics of Militarizing Women's Lives* (Berkeley: University of California Press, 2000); Mary Louise Roberts, *What Soldiers Do: Sex and the American GI in World War II France* (Chicago: University of Chicago Press, 2013).

6. One of the most valuable – and engaging – global country-specific feminist presentations of data on multiple aspects of women's complex lives – divorce, land titles, wages, education, unpaid work, sexual assault – is: Joni Seager, *The Women's Atlas*.

7. Svetlana Alexievich, *The Unwomanly Face of War: An Oral History of Women in World War II* (New York: Random House, 2017, p.58).

8. Wendy Wilder Larsen and Tran Thi Nga, *Shallow Graves: Two Women and Vietnam* (New York: Random House, 1986, pp.211, 219).

9. Marjane Satrapi, *Persepolis* (New York: Pantheon, 2003, p.142).

10. Maaza Mengiste, *The Shadow King* (New York: W W Norton and Company, 2019). Pat Barker, *Silence of the Girls* (New York: Doubleday, 2018). Pat Barker, *The Women of Troy* (New York: Doubleday, 2021).

11. Jill Lepore, *Book of Ages: The Life and Opinions of Jane Franklin* (New York: Alfred A. Knopf, 2013, p.170).

12. Human Rights Watch, *Hopes Betrayed* (New York: Human Rights Watch, 2002). The first person to expose the sex trafficking and forced prostitution system in Bosnia, with its male peacekeepers and contracted police officers among its clients, was an American police officer, Kathryn Bolkovac, herself in Bosnia under contract with the US security company DynCorp. Bolkovac's evidence was ignored by her DynCorp superiors and by several UN officials stationed in post-war Sarajevo. Madeleine Rees, then serving in Sarajevo as the deputy of Mary Robinson, the UN High Commissioner for Human Rights, was one of the few UN officials to provide support for Bolkovac and her claims of trafficking: Kathryn Bolkovac, *The Whistleblower: Sex Trafficking, Military Contractors, and One Woman's Fight for Justice* (New York: Palgrave, 2011).

13. Maryam did not survive: Declan Walsh, "Trapped Between Drought and Extremists" in *New York Times* International Edition, November 23, 2022. A scholarly book exploring the experiences of war for women in a wide range of countries is: Robin Chandler, Linda K Fuller and Lihua Wang, eds, *Women, War and Violence* (New York: Palgrave Macmillan, 2010).

Chapter Two: Every War Is Fought in Gendered History

14. Sarah Kamal, "Disconnected: Women's Radio Listening in Rural Samangan, Afghanistan" in Working Paper #27, Cambridge, MA, MIT Comparative Media Studies, February 15, 2004.

15. Population Reference Bureau, "Afghan Women and Men Far Apart in Literacy" on www.prb.org, June 1, 2000, accessed November 1, 2022.

16. Women Count, "Afghanistan" on www.data.UNwomen.org, February, 2021, accessed November 1, 2022. This was five months before the Taliban re-took state power in Afghanistan.

17. We are continuing to uncover the racially, regionally and class diverse histories of women in industrial paid work during wars. Among the feminist studies of British and US women's paid work during World Wars I and II are: Sherna Berger Gluck, *Rosie the Riveter Revisited: Women, the War, and Social Change* (New York: Meridian Books, 1988); Maureen Honey, *Creating Rosie the Riveter: Class, Gender and Propaganda During World War II* (Amherst, MA: University of Massachusetts Press, 1984); Cynthia Enloe, *Does Khaki Become You?* (London: Pandora Press, 1988); Angela Woollacott, *On Her Their Lives Depend: Munitions Workers in the Great War* (Berkeley: University of California Press, 1994); Penny Summerfield, *Women Workers in the Second World War* (London: Routledge, 2014).

18. A recent book investigating diverse women's suffrage movements is Lucy Delap, *Feminisms: A Global History* (London: Penguin Books, 2020). On Egyptian women's suffrage campaigning, see: Margot Badran, *Feminists, Islam, and Nation: Gender and the Making of Modern Egypt* (Princeton: Princeton University Press, 1995).

19. Council of Europe, *The Four Pillars of the Istanbul Convention,* 2021. www.coe.int, accessed December 12, 2022.

20. Binaifer Norowjee, *Shattered Lives,* Washington, DC, Human Rights Watch, 1996. No page numbers.

21. Christine Chinkin, Women's Initiatives for Gender Justice, 'Toward the Tokyo Tribunal 2000' on www.4genderjustice.org, accessed October 25, 2022.

Chapter Three: Getting Men to Fight Isn't So Easy

22. Anton Troianovski, "Draft Provokes Rising Anguish in Rural Russia" in *New York Times,* September 24, 2022. See also: Gulnaz Sharafutdinova, "Many Russians Are Afraid, But They Still Support Putin" in *New York Times, International Edition,* October 28, 2022. Sharafutdinova is a Russia specialist at Kings College London. Her newest book is *The Afterlife of the 'Soviet Man': Rethinking Homo Sovieticus* (London: Bloomsbury, 2023). For a valuable analysis of Vladimir Putin's own attempts to manipulate ideas and practices of manliness – and Russian feminists' reactions to those efforts – see: Valerie Sperling, *Sex, Politics, and Putin: Political Legitimacy in Russia* (New York and London: Oxford University Press, 2015).

23. Dan Sabbagh, "Russia Says First 82,000 Conscripts from Emergency Draft Sent to Fight" in *Guardian,* October 29, 2022.

24. For graphic details about Russian men's experiences in the Soviet-Afghanistan war and their families' reception of their sons' zinc-welded-closed coffins, see Belarusian, Nobel Prize-winning author Svetlana Alexievich, *Zinky Boys: Soviet Voices from the Afghanistan War* (New York: W.W. Norton and Company, 1992); in the UK: *Boys in Zink* (London: Penguin Books, 1992). For a fascinating interview-based investigation of Russian male veterans' views of their military experiences and post-war conditions following deployment in Chechnya, see Maya Eichler, *Militarizing Men: Gender, Conscription, and War in Post-Soviet Russia* (Stanford: Stanford University Press, 2011).

25. A captured Russian ex-convict recruited in 2023 into the Russian forces interviewed in: Andrew E Kramer, "Sent Forth by Russia as Cannon Fodder, Then Captured by Ukraine" in *New York Times*, February 14, 2023. The journalist used multiple sources to confirm the credibility of this account.

26. Quoting a Russian woman who spoke to journalists anonymously out of fear of reprisals: Anatoly Kurmanaev, Alina Lobzina and Ekaterina Bodyagina, "Back From War, Convict Fighters Will Test Russia" in *New York Times,* January 30, 2023. For the role of Wagner Group military cemeteries in its recruitment strategy, see Christiaan Triebert and Dmitriy Khavin, "A Cemetery in Russia for Mercenaries is Rapidly Expanding" in *New York Times,* January 27, 2023. For confirmed reports on the experiences of men recruited by the Wagner Group to serve as cannon fodder and how people in their Russian home villages received their dead bodies: Francesca Ebel "'Dear Vladimir Vladimirovich' – Russian Conscripts Decry 'Criminal Orders'" in *Washington Post*, March 19, 2023: washingtonpost.com, accessed March 20, 2023; Carlotta Gall, "'This Hell is Close Combat': Casualties Soar in the Fight for Bakhmut" in *New York Times*, March 20, 2023; Neil MacFarquhar, "They Left Town as Convicts. Will They Be Buried as Heroes?" in *New York Times*, March 27, 2023.

27. Anatoly Kurmanaev, "Russia Installs New War Leader Amid Dissension in Putin's Circle" in *New York Times*, January 12, 2023. Further evidence that the Warner Group was relying on prison recruits surfaced when one of those prisoner enlistees sought asylum in Norway: Anatoly Kurmanaev, Henrik Pryser Libell and Michael Schwartz, "Russian Mercenary Defects, and Says He Can Help Inquiry into War Crimes" in *New York Times,* January 18, 2023.

28. Ruth Maclean, Elian Peltier and Eric Schmitt, "France's Troops Soon to Leave Burkina Faso, A Former Ally" in *New York Times,* January

26, 2023. In January 2023, the UN High Commissioner's Office for Human Rights released a report by its team of independent experts, led by Sorcha MacLeod, on possible war crimes, including rape committed by soldiers of the Wagner Group with the soldiers of the government of Mali against civilians, especially from the Fulani, a minority group in Mali: UN Office of the High Commissioner for Human Rights, "Mali: UN Experts Call for Independent Investigation Into Possible International Crimes Committed by Government Forces and 'Wagner Group'" on www.ohchr.org, January 31, 2023, accessed February 2, 2023.

29. By the end of the eleventh month of Putin's war in Ukraine, an estimated 35,000 Russians had sought political asylum in the US alone. No gender breakdown among these asylum-seekers has been given, but it was thought that the majority were Russian men seeking to escape the Russian military's male conscription drive: Mike Baker, "A Daring Quest to Flee Russia, By Motorboat" in *New York Times,* January 29, 2023. The Ukrainian government's fighting force also accepted foreign male fighters, including men from Britain, the US and Belarus. Russian male pro-Ukraine volunteer soldiers were organized into their own unit under a Ukrainian commander. All of these pro-Ukraine uniformed foreign fighters, trainers and rescue workers seemed to be male. See, for instance: Michael Schwirtz, "A Russian Legion Fights Against Its Homeland" in *New York Times,* February 13, 2023.

30. One of the recent detailed historical accounts of the dreadful conditions that men of the British, French, Canadian and German militaries endured, trapped in the seemingly endless trench warfare of World War II, is Mary Louise Roberts, *Sheer Misery: Soldiers in Battle in WWII* (Chicago: Chicago University Press, 2021).

31. Among the relatively few studies of U.S. military prostitution are: Katherine Moon, *Sex Among Allies: Military Prostitution in U.S.-Korea Relations* (New York: Columbia University Press, 1997); Saundra Sturdevant and Brenda Stoltzfus, *Let the Good Times Poll: Prostitution and the U.S. Military in Asia* (New York: The New Press, 1992); Mary Louise Roberts, *What Soldiers Do: Sex and the American GI in World War II France* (Chicago: Chicago University Press, 2013). I have explored militaries' changing policies and practices of prostitution in: Cynthia Enloe, *Maneuvers: The Militarization of Women's Lives* (Berkeley: University of California Press, 2000) and in *Bananas, Beaches and Bases,* second edition (Berkeley: University of California Press, 2014).

32. Siobhán O'Grady and Anastacia Galouchka, "The Letters Left Behind by Soldiers Demoralized Russian Soldiers As They Fled" in *Washington Post,* September 15, 2022. I am grateful to my colleague, Russian poli-

tics gender specialist Valerie Sperling, for helping me decipher these meanings.

33. My own effort to explore dozens of militaries' ethnicized and racialized recruitment, promotion and deployment strategies is *Ethnic Soldiers: State Security in Divided Societies* (London: Penguin Books, 1980). While I learned a lot from doing the research, this earlier investigation is embarrassingly lacking in gender analysis. For a study of the everyday experiences of diverse masculinities in the British army: Victoria Basham, *War, Identity and the Liberal State: Everyday Experiences of the Geopolitical in the Armed Forces* (London and New York: Routledge, 2013).

34. Cynthia Enloe, "The Recruiter and the Skeptic" in *Critical Military Studies,* vol. 1, no. 1, 2015, pp.3–10.

35. An investigation into the British government's efforts to muster civilian women's support for British soldiers during the British military involvement in both the Afghanistan and Iraq wars is: Katharine M Millar, *Support the Troops: Military Obligation, Gender, and the Making of Political Community* (London and New York: Oxford University Press, 2022). The lives and ideas of women as the wives of British male soldiers during these same conflicts are explored in a feminist ethnography: Alex Hyde, *Regimented Life: An Ethnography of Army Wives* (Edinburgh: University of Edinburgh Press, 2023).

36. The British Ministry of Defence today is facing angry complaints from military wives who charge the ministry and its private contractors with failing to repair their houses' leaks and rot. The Ministry admitted that poor housing was among the causes for soldiers' refusing to re-enlist: Daniel Boffey, "Third of Military Homes Still in Bad State Despite Repair Contracts" in *Guardian*, November 7, 2022.

37. Among other recent studies exploring the lives of women married to soldiers are: Vron Ware, *Military Migrants: Fighting for YOUR Country* (London: Palgrave, 2012); Amanda Chisholm, *The Gendered and Colonial Lives of Gurkhas in Private Security: From Military to Market* (Edinburgh: University of Edinburgh Press, 2022). Chisholm reveals the assessments and coping strategies of Nepalese women married to men enlisted in Gurkha regiments and Gurkha-hiring private security companies. For the calculations that wives of men in private security forces make, see Maya Eichler, ed., *Gender and Private Security in Global Politics* (London: Oxford University Press, 2015). See also: Maria Eriksson Baaz and Judith Verweijen, "The Agency of Liminality: Army Wives in the Democratic Republic of the Congo and the Tactical Reversal of Militarization" in *Critical Military Studies*, vol. 3, no. 3, December, 2017, pp.267–86. My own investigations of diverse women as military

wives – and governments' attempts to control them – began with *Does Khaki Become You?* (London: Pluto Press, 1983; Boston: South End Press, 1983), and then deepened in later books: *Maneuvers* (Berkeley: University of California Press, 2000) and *Nimo's War, Emma's War: Making Feminist Sense of the Iraq War* (Berkeley: University of California Press, 2010).

38. I learned more of American mothers' and wives' activism while researching *Nimo's War, Emma's War: Making Feminist Sense of the Iraq War* (Berkeley: University of California Press, 2010). Russian women's purchasing military gear for their male family members is described in Pjotr Sauer, "Mobilised Russian Left to Bid Online for Vital Kit" in *Guardian*, October 21, 2022; Neil MacFarquhar, "'Coffins Are Already Coming': The Toll of Russia's Chaotic Draft" in *New York Times*, International Edition, October 19, 2022.

39. A scholarly analysis of the Soldiers' Mothers movement is: *Saving Russia's Sons: The Soldiers' Mothers and the Russian-Chechen Wars* (Manchester: Manchester University Press, 2008). For an analysis of how the Soldiers' Mothers' organizing challenged government-fostered nationalism, militarism and patriotism, see also: Valerie Sperling, "The Last Refuge of a Scoundrel: Patriotism, Militarism and the Russian National Idea" in *Nations and Nationalism*, vol. 9, 2003, pp.235–53. *Warning:* in an effort to disempower the Soldiers' Mothers independent civil society movement – and as a testimony to the government's nervousness – the Russian government created a "copycat" pro-government, pro-war organization that it deceptively calls "Committee of Soldiers' Mothers." In reaction, the original women activists renamed their authentically critical group: "Union of Committees of Soldiers' Mothers." I am grateful to Valerie Sperling for sharing this crucial information with me.

40. In November 2022, the Putin-dominated Russian parliament passed a law expanding already stiff legal penalties for promoting "non-traditional sexual relationships": Pjotr Sauer, "MPs Pass Law Criminalizing all 'LGBT Propaganda,'" in *Guardian*, November 25, 2022.

41. Andrew Roth, "Kremlin Audience with Putin is Whitewash, Say Families of Conscripts" in *Guardian*, November 24, 2022.

42. Vladimir Putin was quoted in an extensive special section of *New York Times*: Michael Schwirtz, Anton Troianovski, Yousur Al-Hlou, Masha Froliak, Adam Entous, Thomas Gibbons-Neff, "Putin's War" in *New York Times*, December 18, 2022. Also reporting on this meeting of selected soldiers' mothers with Putin: Andrew Roth and Pjotr Sauer, "'There are Many Lies,' Putin Tells Gathering of Soldiers' Mothers Chosen by Kremlin" in *Guardian*, November 26, 2022.

43. Ibid., Putin quoted in Schwirtz, et al.
44. Valerie Hopkins, "Russian City Mourns Dead But Supports the War" in *New York Times,* December 28, 2022.
45. This account is from: Neil MacFarquhar and Alina Lobzina, "'Give Back Their Bodies'" in *New York Times, International Edition,* November 8, 2022.

Chapter Four: Women as Soldiers Is Not Liberation

46. Daniel Boffey, "Only [*sic*] 20% of Rape Charges Tried by Court Martial End in No Conviction" in *Guardian,* November 3, 2022.
47. Aoife Walsh and Victoria Lindrea, "Royal Navy Investigates after Women Come Forward with Abuse Claims", BBC, October 29, 2022: www.bbc.com/news/uk-63435129, accessed December 18, 2022.
48. Sarah Bell, "Female Royal Navy Sailor 'Was Raped on Ship'", BBC News, November 10, 2022: www.bbc.com/news/uk-63556169, accessed December 18, 2022. Between 2019 and 2021, the British Royal Navy's submarine justice system heard fifty-three charges of rape. Only eleven of those ended in convictions of the accused rapist. Daniel Boffey, "Only [*sic*] 20% of Rape Charges Tried by Court Martial End in No [*sic*] Conviction" in *Guardian,* November 3, 2022.
49. After studying militaries for a decade, I only belatedly realized that if I was going to fully understand military politics I would have to take nurses seriously: Cynthia Enloe, *Does Khaki Become You?* (London: Pluto Press, 1983; Boston: South End Press, 1983). A follow-up study of militarized nurses is: Cynthia Enloe, *Maneuvers* (Berkeley: University of California Press, 2000).
50. "Unsung Heroes: Women of World War II" (London: Royal Mail, 2022).
51. Megan MacKenzie, *Beyond the Band of Brothers: The US Military and the Myth that Women Can't Fight* (New York and Cambridge: Cambridge University Press, 2015). I began tracking the gendered contest over "combat" in the early 1980s with *Does Khaki Become You? The Militarization of Women's Lives* (London: Pluto Press, 1983; Boston: South End Press, 1983), and continued my tracking in *Maneuvers* (Berkeley: University of California Press, 2000), and *Globalization and Militarism: Feminists Make the Link* (Lanham, MD: Rowman & Littlefield, second edition, 2016).
52. Cynthia Enloe, *The Morning After: Sexual Politics at the End of the Cold War* (Berkeley: University of California Press, 1993).
53. I explored this practice in *The Morning After* (Berkeley: University of California Press, 1993). Aaron Belkin and the San Francisco-based Palm

Center, which he directed, sponsored the most thorough cross-national research projects that revealed that governments lifting the gay ban did not hurt military effectiveness.

54. I am grateful to Ellie Beargeon, herself an LGBTQ US army veteran and feminist researcher, for tutoring me in the realities of today's apparently gay-friendly US military. Her MA thesis based on interviews with racially diverse recent LGBTQ veterans is: Ellie Beargeon, "'Diverse Warriors': Experiences of Recruitment, Enlistment and Service in the United States Armed Forces, 2011–2021," unpublished MA thesis, Department of International Development, Environment and Community, Clark University, Worcester, MA, 2019.

55. Out of these discussions came a small but provocative book: Wendy Chapkis, ed., *Loaded Questions: Women in the Military* (Amsterdam: Transnational Institute, 1981).

56. For unusual personal descriptions of what it is like to be a teenage Eritrean girl conscripted into the Eritrean military, see: Ruta Yosef-Tudla, "I'm Against War on Principle," and Bisrat Habte Micael, "I've Had Enough of War," in Ellen Elster and Majken Jul Sorensen, eds, *Women and Conscientious Objection: An Anthology* (London: War Resisters International, 2010).

57. An especially nuanced study of the ethnically gendered dynamics that shape the Israeli military is: Edna Lomsky Feder and Orna Sasson-Levy, *Women Soldiers and Citizenship in Israel* (New York: Routledge, 2018). Fumika Sato, Professor at Tokyo's Hitotsubashi University, is the principal researcher focused on women in the Japanese Defense Forces. See, for instance: Sato, "The 'Benevolent' Japan Self-Defense Forces and Their Utilization of Women" in *Hitotsubashi Journal of Social Sciences*, vol. 51, January, 2020, pp.1–23. For an analysis of the South African military's gender politics at the end of Apartheid, see: Jacklyn Cock, *Women and War in South Africa* (Cleveland, OH: Pilgrim Press, 1993). The most complete cross-branch, rank-specific and racially comparative accounting of women in the US military is: Lory Manning, *Women in the Military: Where They Stand* (Washington, DC: Women's Research and Education Institute, eighth edition, 2013). Manning's report is a model. Since WREI closed its doors, there has not been such a thorough report on women in the US military. Moreover, I am not aware of any similarly ambitious reporting on where women are – by branch, job, rank, and by race and ethnicity – in any of the world's state militaries.

58. For a clear analysis of the dynamics of the Ethiopian 2021–22 war and Eritrea's role in it, see the commentary by Ero Comfort, the first woman to head the influential NGO, the International Crisis Group: "Biden Must Ensure Ethiopia Does Not Return to War" in Opinion, *New York*

Times, International Edition, November 13, 2022. Ero Comfort has spent years working in African war and post-war zones.

59. A collection of Teaiwa's writings – poetry, research-based articles and critical essays – is: Teresia Teaiwa, *Sweat and Salt Water: Selected Works* (Honolulu: University of Hawaii Press, 2021).

60. This reminds me of one of the best-ever book titles: *All the Blacks are Men, All the Women are White, But Some of Us are Brave: Black Feminist Studies,* (Albany, Kitchen Table Press, 1982), edited by Barbara Smith and her Black feminist colleagues.

61. One of the most celebrated – especially within the African American community – Black female units in US military history was the US Army's World War II-era 6888th postal unit. The history of the women in this unit, the only African American women soldiers to be deployed outside the US during World War II, is: Brenda L Moore, *To Serve My Country, To Serve My Race: The Story of the Only African-American WACS Stationed Overseas During World War II* (New York: New York University Press, 1996). For an interesting comparison, see: Ben Bousquet and Colin Douglas, *West Indian Women at War: British Racism in World War II* (London: Lawrence and Wishart, 1991). Both Bousquet's and Douglas's mothers had served in West Indian women's British military units.

62. The principal advocacy group for women in the US military is SWAN: Service Women's Action Network: www.servicewomensactionnetwork.org

63. The official re-investigation of the Tailhook convention forced on the Navy by the late Congresswoman Pat Schroeder and her colleagues was published as a commercial book and remains a valuable guide to the workings of masculinized patriarchy: US Department of the Navy, *The Tailhook Report: The Official Inquiry into the Events of Tailhook '91* (New York: St. Martin's Press, 2000).

64. Megan MacKenzie explores the dynamics through which American, Canadian and Australian publics continue to respect their militaries, despite repeated sexual scandals in each of these forces: Megan MacKenzie, *Good Soldiers Don't Rape* (Cambridge: Cambridge University Press, 2023). A US woman veteran's candid account of her own experiences of sexism and sexual assault – and her speaking out about both – when she served in the Marine Corps is: Anuradha Bhagwati, *Unbecoming: A Memoir of Disobedience* (New York and London: Atria, 2019). The official investigation by a former Canadian Supreme Court Justice into male personnel's sexual harassment and assaults on women within the Canadian military is: Louise Arbour, *Independent External Comprehensive Review into Sexual Misconduct and Sexual Harassment* (Ottawa: Canadian Ministry of Defense, 2022). I am grateful to Professor

Maya Eichler for inviting me to take part in a conversation with Canadian military women trying to explain and stop sexual abuse in the forces: Mount Saint Vincent University, Halifax, Nova Scotia, February 2023. In December 2022, an alliance of members of the US Congress, led by NY Democrat Senator Kirsten Gillibrand, succeeded to push through legislation (a seemingly small item within the huge US Congressional bill financing the US Defense Department) taking authority over investigating sexual assaults within the US armed forces out of the hands of military commanders and assigning that authority to independent prosecutors, a move women's advocates believed would reduce the impunity too often granted to military men accused of sexually assaulting other military men and military women: Catie Edmondson, "Military Bill Voiding Rule for Vaccines is Cleared" in *New York Times,* December 16, 2022. Shirley Graham, an Irish gender scholar, has detailed how Irish military senior officers tried to prevent her from exposing the sexist culture experienced by women in the Irish Defense Forces: Shirley Graham, "The Irish Defense Forces and the Silencing of a Feminist Researcher" in *Critical Military Studies,* December, 2022: doi.org/10.10 80/23337486.2022.2156840. See also Karina Molloy, *A Woman in Defense: A Soldier's Story of the Enemy Within the Irish Army* (Dublin: Hatchett Books Ireland, 2023).

65. Phoebe Donnelly, Dyan Mazurana and Evyn Papworth, *Blue on Blue: Investigating Sexual Abuse of Peacekeepers* (New York: International Peace Institute, 2022). For a densely researched study of race, gender and sexuality in international peacekeeping operations and host country's civilian men's and women's engagements with those mostly male peacekeepers, see Marsha Henry, *Critical Interventions: The Gendered, Racialized, Militarized Politics of Peacekeeping* (Philadelphia: Penn University Press, 2023).

66. Ibid., Donnelly, Mazurana and Papworth, p.14.

67. Ibid., p.13.

Chapter Five: Women as Armed Insurgents Offer Feminist Caveats

68. A novel evoking the Trung sisters is: E M Tran, *Daughters of the New Year* (New York: Hanover Square Press, 2022).

69. A joint collection of writings by Vietnamese and US gender specialists derived from this 1993 trip: Kathleen Barry, ed., *Vietnam's Women in Transition* (New York: St Martin's Press, 1996). See also: Hue-Tam Ho Tai, *Radicalism and the Origins of the Vietnamese Revolution* (Cambridge, MA: Harvard University Press, 1992).

70. I am grateful to historian Karen Turner for tutoring me in these harsh gendered realities. Her interview-based book study: Karen Gottschang Turner with Phan Thanh Hao, *Even the Women Must Fight: Memories of War from North Vietnam* (Boston: John Wiley and Sons, 1999).

71. Australian Human Rights Institute and the Vietnam Center for Gender Studies and Leadership, Ho Chi Minh National Academy of Politics, "New Research into the Status of Women in Vietnam's Political System" (Sydney: University of New South Wales, 2022): www.humanrights.unsw. edu.au/news/new-research-status-women-vietnams-political-system.

72. Among the earliest studies to explore the question "what happened?" cross-nationally through a gender lens is: Sonia Kruks, Rayna Rapp and Marilyn B Young, eds, *Promissory Notes: Women in the Transition to Socialism* (New York: Monthly Review Press, 1989).

73. A thoughtful interview-based study of the ongoing reflective assessments of Cuban insurgent women in the gender dynamics shaping the Fidel Castro-led 1950s revolution, in which they themselves played an important part, is Lorraine Bayard de Volo, *Women and the Cuban Insurrection: How Gender Shaped Castro's Victory* (Cambridge and New York: Cambridge University Press, 2018).

74. A careful, ethnographic study of women in the insurgent Turkish-Kurdish PKK is: Isabel Käser, *The Kurdish Women's Freedom Movement: Gender, Body Politics and Militant Femininities* (Cambridge and New York: Cambridge University Press, 2021). A notably collaborative study by women scholars and activists into Myanmar ethnically diverse women's resistance efforts is: Jenny Hedström and Elisabeth Olivius, eds, *Waves of Upheaval in Myanmar: Gendered Transformations and Political Transitions* (Copenhagen: Nordic Institute of Asian Studies (NIAS) Press, 2022).

75. One of the most prominent studies of women in fundamentalist and terrorist armed groups – and how they are portrayed – is: Caron E Gentry and Laura Sjoberg, *Beyond Mothers, Monsters and Whores: Thinking about Women's Violence in Global Politics* (London: Zed Books, 2015).

76. Women's incentives for joining armed groups in Ukraine, Colombia and the Kurdish regions of the Middle East are explored in Jessica Trisko Darden, Alexis Henshaw and Ora Szekely, *Insurgent Women: Female Combatants in Civil Wars* (Washington, DC: Georgetown University Press, 2019). For women's experiences in the insurgent Huk rebellion in the Philippines, see: Vina Lanzona, *Amazons of the Huk Rebellion: Gender, Sex, and Revolution in the Philippines* (Madison: University of Wisconsin Press, 2009). For the stories of Mexican women active in the rebellious Zapatista movement of the 1990s, see: Hilary Klein,

Companeras: Zapatista Women's Stories (New York: Seven Stories Press, 2015); Northern Ireland's Protestant women's experiences in the Loyalist paramilitary is explored in: Sandra McEvoy, "Loyalist Women Paramilitaries in Northern Ireland," *Security Studies*, vol. 18, 2009, pp.262–86. Northern Irish women's experiences in the nationalist IRA rebellion and since the Good Friday peace agreement are analyzed in: Niall Gilmartin, *Female Combatants After Armed Struggle: Lost in Transition?* (London and New York: Routledge, 2018).

77. The results of this Helsinki gathering are published in: Eva Isaksson, ed., *Women and the Military System* (London and New York: Harvester-Wheatsheaf, 1988).

78. Marie-Aimée Hélie-Lucas, "The Role of Women during the Algerian Liberation Struggle and After: Nationalism as Concept and Practice Towards Both the Power of the Army and the Militarization of the People" in Isaksson, ed., *Women and the Military System*, p.171.

79. Ibid., pp.184–5. In 1984, Marie-Aimée Hélie-Lucas, by then in exile from Algeria, founded the transnational feminist network, Women Living Under Muslim Laws, to document and analyze those government laws restricting women's rights that were justified by a political elite's melding of religious and nationalist forms of patriarchy.

80. The books that Margaret Randall has written based on her interviews with Sandinista women insurgents are: *Sandino's Daughters* (Vancouver: New Star Books, 1981); *Sandino's Daughters Revisited: Feminism in Nicaragua* (New Brunswick, NJ: Rutgers University Press, 1994). Among Margaret Randall's books on Cuban insurgent women is: *Women in Cuba* (Smyrna, NY: Smyrna Press, 1981).

81. These and other quotations from the 1979 interviews are from Margaret Randall, *Sandino's Daughters.*

82. These quotes from Michele Najlis are from Margaret Randall, *Sandino's Daughters Revisited,* pp.56–7.

83. Detailed accounts of ethnically diverse Myanmar rural and urban women's lives during decades of war, as well as the current post-coup war in Myanmar, are collected in: Jenny Hedström and Elisabeth Olivius, eds, *Waves of Upheaval: Political Transitions and Gendered Transformations in Myanmar* (Copenhagen: Nordic Institute of Asian Studies (NIAS) Press, 2022).

84. Hannah Beech, "Taking on Myanmar Generals, Women Emerge as 'True Warriors'" in *New York Times*, March 5, 2021.

85. Hannah Beech interviewed by Michael Barbaro, "A Military That Kills Its Own People," in *New York Times*, April 8, 2021.

86. Hannah Beech, "Confronting a Military Coup: 'I Will Die Protecting My Country'" in *New York Times*, March 25, 2021.

87. I am indebted to my colleague Parissara (Gai) Liewkeat, Thai feminist and international civil servant, who over the past twenty-five years has shared with me a series of reports that Kachin, Karen and Shan women have published to document the Myanmar military's wielding of sexual violence in its war against minority communities. See also Jenny Hedström and Elisabeth Olivius, eds, *Waves of Upheaval.*

Chapter Six: Wounds Matter – Wounds Are Gendered

88. In early 2023, six decades after the Korean War, a debate broke out in Washington over the inaccuracies of the names, even their total number, to be chiseled on a new memorial due to be erected on the Washington Mall to commemorate just the Americans who died in that war: Dave Philipps, "Korean War Memorial is Riddled with Errors" in *New York Times,* January 9, 2023.

89. A belated attempt to rectify British officials' earlier deliberate steps to undercount the deaths of men they recruited from Britain's colonies to wage World War I is: Commonwealth War Graves Commission, *Report of the Special Committee to Review Historical Inequalities in Commemoration* (Maidenhead, UK: The Commonwealth War Graves Commission, 2021).

90. After just the first eleven months of war in Ukraine, intelligence agencies estimated that Russian state and mercenary forces had suffered "dead and wounded" amounting to 200,000 soldiers. The proportions of the total who were wounded and the nature of their wounds was not tallied: Helene Cooper, Eric Schmitt and Thomas Gibbons-Neff, "War Dead and Neat 200,000 for Russia" in *New York Times,* February 3, 2023. One of the most ambitious research projects tallying the myriad human, material and financial costs of any war is the Costs of War Project at Brown University, co-founded in 2011 by anthropologist Catherine Lutz, who currently co-directs the project with political scientist Neta Crawford. The project researchers began by trying to do an accounting of the true costs of the US-led war in Iraq, though they currently attempt to include the costs of what its staff now calls the "post-9/11 wars," including the post-2001 wars in Iraq, Pakistan, Afghanistan and Syria: costsofwar@brown.edu. Out of the Costs of War Project has come Catherine Lutz and Andrea Mazzarino, eds, *War and Health: The Medical Consequences of the Wars in Iraq and Afghanistan* (New York: NYU Press, 2019).

91. Claire Armitstead, "Pat Barker: 'You Could Argue that Time's Up: We're at the End of Patriarchy'" in *Guardian,* January 4, 2019. Pat Barker, *The Silence of the Girls* (New York: Anchor Books, 2018); Pat Barker, *The Women of Troy* (New York: Anchor Books, 2021).

92. The exhibit's catalogue, with insightful commentaries, is: Ana Carden-Coyne, David Morris and Tim Wilcox, eds, *The Sensory War: 1914–2014* (Manchester, UK: Manchester Art Gallery, 2014).

93. Among the nuanced studies of the lives of American war-wounded and their domestic carers are: Sarah Hautzinger and Jean Scandlyn, *Beyond Post-Traumatic Stress: Homefront Struggles With the War on Terror* (Walnut Creek, CA: Left Coast Press, 2014); Ann Jones, *They Were Soldiers: How the Wounded Return from America's Wars — The Untold Story* (Chicago: Haymarket Books, 2013); David Finkel, *Thank You for Your Service* (New York: Farrar, Straus and Giroux, 2013). A photographic essay of Ukrainian male soldiers suffering mental health trauma in the midst of the war in Ukraine and those men's difficult relationships with the women in their lives is: Ellen Barry, with Antoine d'Agata, photographer, "Voices from Pavlivka: Inside a Psychiatric Hospital in Kyiv" in *New York Times Magazine*, March 19, 2023, pp.18–31.

94. See, for instance: Linda Burnham and Nik Theodore, *The Invisible and Unregulated World of Domestic Work* (New York: National Domestic Workers Alliance, 2012); Naila Kabeer, Ratna Sudarshan and Kirsty Milward, eds, *Organizing Women in the Informal Economy* (London: Zed Books, 2013); Merike Blofield, *Care Work and Class: Domestic Workers' Struggles for Equal Rights in Latin America* (University Park: Penn State University Press, 2013); Cynthia Enloe, "Scrubbing the Globalized Tub: Domestic Servants in World Politics" in Chapter 8, *Bananas, Beaches and Bases,* second edition (Berkeley: University of California Press, 2014); Jennifer N Fish, *Domestic Workers of the World Unite!* (New York: NYU Press, 2017).

95. The Florence Nightingale Museum is located on the grounds of the St Thomas Hospital, Lambeth Place, London.

96. Drawing on Florence Nightingale's extensive correspondence, biographer Gillian Gill offers a detailed account of her medical work in the Crimea: *Nightingales: Florence and her Fmaily* (New York: Random House, 2005). Mary Seacole, the Jamaican traveler, businesswoman and natural healer who established a drinks-and-healthcare center for British soldiers serving in Crimea, is the subject of a new biography: Helen Rappaport, *In Search of Mary Seacole: The Making of a Cultural Icon* (London: Simon & Schuster, 2022). Together, the histories of Nightingale and Seacole expose the conditions under which British male soldiers served during the 1850s Crimean War.

97. Mark Piesing, "The Deadly Danger You Can't See" on BBC, March 22, 2017: www.bbc.com/future/article/20170321-the-deadly-danger-you-cant-see, accessed December 28, 2022. See also the website of the International Campaign to Ban Land mines: icbl.org.

98. Hana Salama and Emma Bjertén-Günther, *Women Managing Weapons* (Geneva: United Nations Institute for Disarmament Research (UNIDIR), 2021).

99. Maria Varenikova, "Solace in Ukraine's Forests, Despite the Peril" in *New York Times,* International Edition, December 6, 2022.

100. Alex Horton, "Ukraine Combat Amputees Face a Hard Road Home" on *Washington Post,* December 18, 2022: www.washingtonpost.com, accessed December 18, 2022.

101. Zoë Wool, *After War: The Weight of Life at Walter Reed* (Durham, NC: Duke University Press, 2015). My own efforts to describe and analyze the gendered politics of wartime amputations are in *Nimo's War, Emma's War*: "Charlene," Chapter 9, which describes the maternal labor performed by an American woman whose son lost his leg in the Iraq war, and "Danielle," Chapter 7, which tells of an African American woman soldier and former athlete who lost her hand in the same war.

102. Alex Horton, "Ukraine Combat Amputees Face a Hard Road Home", on *Washington Post,* December 18, 2022: www.washingtonpost.com, accessed December 18, 2022. See also: Eric Nagourney, "Path to Heal Has a Stop in the U.S." in *New York Times*, March 25, 2023.

Chapter Seven: Make Wartime Rape Visible

103. Jacqui True, Australian feminist scholar, has investigated the dynamics of violence against women in multiple areas of armed conflict: Jacqui True, *Violence Against Women: What Everyone Needs to Know* (London: Oxford University Press, 2020).

104. Dyan Mazurana, et al., *What "Rape As a Weapon of War" in Tigray Really Means*, on World Peace Foundation, August 10, 2021: tufts. edu/reinventingpeace, accessed September 30, 2022. Also see: Amnesty International, *Ethiopia: Troops and Militia Rape, Abduct Women and Girls in Tigray,* on Amnesty International, August 10, 2021: www.amnesty.org/en/latest/news/2021/08/ethiopia-troops-and-militia-rape-abduct-women-and-girls-in-tigray, accessed January 6, 2023. Dyan Mazurana and her research colleagues have investigated what has happened to those girls and boys born to women who endured rape in wartime: Kimberly Theidon, Dyan Mazurana, and Dipali Anumol, eds, *Challenging Conceptions: Children Born of Wartime Rape and Sexual Exploitation* (New York and London: Oxford University Press, 2023).

105. Daclan Walsh, "After Secret U.S. Talks Fail, A Hidden War in Africa Rapidly Escalates" in *New York Times,* October 8, 2022.

106. Among the scholars who have investigated the masculinities of wartime male rapists is Inger Skjelsbæk, *The Political Psychology of War Rape: Studies from Bosnia and Herzegovina* (London and NY: Routledge, 2011). Inger Skjelsbæk is one of the founders of the gender analysis section of the Peace Research Institute Oslo (PRIO). My own modest effort to understand one male wartime rapist and how he was influenced by other men is: "All the Men are in Militias, All the Women are Victims: The Politics of Masculinity and Femininity in Nationalist Wars," Chapter 7, in Cynthia Enloe, *The Curious Feminist* (Berkeley: University of California Press, 2004, pp.99–118).

107. A rare social science investigation of male-on-male rape inside a state military is: Insook Kwon, "Sexual Violence Among Men in the Military in South Korea" on *Journal of Interpersonal Violence*, 2004, journals. sagepub.com/doi/abs/10.1177/0886260507302998.

108. Ximena Bunster, "Surviving Beyond Fear: Women and Torture in Latin America," in June Nash and Helen I Safa, eds, *Women and Change in Latin America* (South Hadley, MA: Bergin and Garvey, 1986, pp.297–325). A recent collection of essays analyzing how torture is portrayed and perceived is: Rory Cox, Faye Donnelly and Anthony F Lang, eds, *Contesting Torture: Interdisciplinary Perspectives* (London and New York: Routledge, 2022).

109. *Calling the Ghosts*, documentary film directed by Karmen Jelincic and Mandy Jacobson (New York: Women Make Movies, 1996).

110. See, for instance, Chunghee Sarah Soh, "The Korean 'Comfort Women': Movement for Redress" in *Asian Survey,* vol. 36, no. 12, December 1996, pp.1226–40; Na-Young Lee, "The Korean Women's Movement of Japanese 'Comfort Women'," in Carole E McCann, et al., eds, *Feminist Theory Reader: Local and Global Perspectives* (London and New York: Routledge, 2020).

111. Michèle Midori Fillion, director, *No Job for a Woman* (New York: Women Make Movies, 2011).

112. Elizabeth Becker, *You Don't Belong Here: How Three Women Rewrote the Story of War* (New York: Public Affairs, 2021).

113. My own personal favorite accounts of women organizing to challenge the sexism of news media organizations are: Nan Robertson, *The Girls in the Balcony: Women, Men, and the* New York Times (New York: Random House, 1992); Lynn Povich, *The Good Girls Revolt: How the Women of Newsweek Sued Their Bosses and Changed the Workplace* (New York: Public Affairs, 2012).

114. Wendy Holden quoted by Julie Welch, in *The Fleet Street Girls: The Women Who Broke Down the Doors of the Gentleman's Club* (London:

Trapeze, 2020, p.207). Julie Welch herself was one of the first British women journalists to cover men's soccer.

115. Zahra Hankir, ed., *Our Women on the Ground: Essays by Arab Women Reporting from the Arab World* (New York: Penguin Books, 2019).

116. Reporters Without Borders, "Since the Taliban Takeover, 40% of Afghan Media Have Closed, 80% of Women Journalists Have Lost their Jobs" on RSF, December 2021: rsf.org/en/taliban-takeover-40-afghan-media-have-closed-80-women-journalists-have-lost-their-jobs, accessed June 15, 2022. A beautiful photographic essay of Afghan women living under Taliban rule a year and a half after the Taliban takeover of government includes women journalists and radio producers who were forced to quit their media jobs: Christina Goldbaum, "For Women, Devastation Beyond War" in *New York Times*, March 26, 2023. The photographer is Kiana Hayeri.

117. Sabrina Tavernise, "Aftereffects: Rights and Tolerance; Iraqi Women Wary of New Upheavals" in *New York Times,* May 5, 2003. Nimo, the Baghdad beauty parlor owner, became the inspiration for Chapter 2, "Nimo," in my own work on the war in Iraq, *Nimo's War, Emma's War.*

118. Among the transnational feminist activists who have generously tutored me in the histories of feminist lobbying of treaty-writing diplomats are the late Rhonda Copelon, Charlotte Bunch, Roxanna Carrillo, Lepa Mladjenovic, Carol Cohn, Christine Chinkin, Ray Acheson and Madeleine Rees.

119. The website for The Hague-based Women's Initiatives for Gender Justice is: www.4genderjustice.org.

120. Holly Porter, *After Rape: Violence, Justice, and Social Harmony in Uganda* (Cambridge: Cambridge University Press, 2017). I am also grateful to Holly Porter for our conversations about her years living in Northern Uganda, as we walked through meadows along the river Cam in the fall of 2022. A valuable collection of essays by feminist researchers working to craft genuinely feminist-informed investigative ethics and skills when conducting their research projects in war zones is: Annick T R Wibben, ed., *Researching War: Feminist Methods, Ethics and Politics* (London and New York: Routledge, 2022). A cross-national volume of commentaries on wartime rape is: Gaby Zipfel, Regina Muhlhauser and Kirsten Campbell, eds, *In Plain Sight: Sexual Violence in Armed Conflict* (New Delhi: Zubaan, 2019). Olivera Simic, a legal scholar and Bosnian Serb feminist researcher, has published several studies of the politics of silencing wartime rape survivors, among them: *Silenced Victims of Wartime Sexual Violence*

(London and New York: Routledge, 2019); *Lola's War* (London and New York: Palgrave Macmillan, 2023).

121. The most detailed account of Ida B Wells' long political career investigating and organizing against post-civil war lynching and other forms of racism is Paula J Giddings, *Ida: A Sword Among Lions* (New York: Amistad, 2008).

122. Susan Brownmiller, *Against Our Will: Men, Women and Rape* (New York: Simon & Schuster, 1975).

123. This account is drawn from Carlotta Gall, "Ukraine Finds Evidence of Sex Crimes in Areas Russia Occupied" in *New York Times,* January 6, 2023. I have followed Carlotta Gall's feminist-informed war zone reporting during her time in Afghanistan, Turkey and Ukraine. The *New York Times* photographer for this article was Laura Boushnak.

124. Sohailla Abdulali, *What We Talk About When We Talk About Rape* (Brighton, UK: Myriad Editions, 2018; New York: The New Press, 2018, p.21).

Chapter Eight: Feminists Organize While War Is Raging

125. I am indebted to Elin Berg, a Swedish feminist scholar at the Swedish Defense University, for explaining this gendered selective conscription process to me. She is investigating the current gendered practices of Swedish conscription.

126. Daniel Conway, a South African international gender politics scholar at Westminster University in London, conducted a critical study of the gendered relationships inside the male-led anti-apartheid End Conscription movement in early 1990s South Africa: Daniel Conway, *Masculinities, Militarization and the End Conscription Campaign: War Resistance in Apartheid South Africa* (Manchester, UK: University of Manchester Press, 2012; Johannesburg: Wits University Press, 2012).

127. Insook Kwon, a prominent South Korean feminist and now legislator, has considered where Korean feminists are in the salient politics of male conscription in South Korea: Insook Kwon, "Gender, Feminism and Masculinity in Anti-Militarism: Focusing on the Conscientious Objection Movement in South Korea" in *International Feminist Journal of Politics,* vol. 15, issue 2, 2012, pp.213–33.

128. Ferda Ülker, quoted in: Ellen Elster and Majken Jul Sorensen, eds, *Women and Conscientious Objection: An Anthology* (London: War Resisters International, 2010), www.wri-irg.org/en/pubs/WomenCOs. For a collection of perspectives on conscientious objection see: Özgür

Heval Çinar and Coşkun Üsterçí, eds, *Conscientious Objection: Resisting Militarized Society* (London: Zed Books, 2009).

129. Fawzia Koofi, "The World Is Still Falling for the Taliban's Lies" in *New York Times,* January 21, 2023. One of the feminist transnational groups that supplied training and other support to Afghan women parliamentary candidates is Mina's List: www.minaslist.org. Mina's List also led international efforts to get threatened women MPs to safety after the Taliban takeover. I am grateful to Mina's List founder, Tanya Henderson, for keeping me informed on the continuing organized efforts by Afghan women MPs in exile. For more on the women MPs in exile: Amie Ferris-Rotman, "'We Will Start Again': Afghan Female MPs Fight on from Parliament in Exile" in *Guardian,* November 27, 2021: www.theguardian.com/global-development/2021/nov/27/we-will-start-again-Afghan-female-mps-fight-on, accessed January 14, 2023.

130. I am forever indebted to Lepa Mladjenovic, Staša Zajović, the late-Cynthia Cockburn, Nebahat Akkoc, Ayse Gül Altinay, Madeleine Rees and Tanya Henderson for introducing me to these wartime feminist activists.

131. A British documentary filmmaker has made a film in which contemporary British women researched and then played the parts of actual British women who sought, in 1915, to travel to The Hague to join the Women's Peace Congress: Charlotte Bill, director and producer, *These Dangerous Women* (Clapham, UK: Clapham Film Unit, 2015). The WILPF-Australia branch has offered a short history of the organization's 1915 origins: www.wilpf.org.au.

132. The 1914–1918 wartime tensions among suffragists in just one British town are described in: Sue Slack, *Cambridge Women and the Struggle for the Vote* (Stroud, UK: Amberley Publishing, 2018). British socialist suffragist Sylvia Pankhurst's World War I rejection of pro-war politics – and thus alienation from her mother and sister, Emmeline and Christabel Pankhurst – are detailed in: Rachel Holmes, *Sylvia Pankhurst: Natural Born Rebel* (London: Bloomsbury, 2020, pp.432–57).

133. A wonderfully provocative collection of cross-national studies of women's organizing during World War I is: Alison S Fell and Ingrid Sharp, eds, *Women's Movement in Wartime: International Perspectives, 1914–19* (London: Palgrave Macmillan, 2007).

134. Louis P Lochner, "International Peace Congress of Women" in *The Advocate for Peace*, vol. 77, no. 7, July 1915: www.jstor.org/stable/20667269, accessed January 10, 2023.

135. "WILPF Resolutions, 1st Congress, The Hague, Netherlands, 1915" in The Women's International League for Peace and Freedom (WILPF)

Archives, Fawcett Library, London, London School of Economics: www.wilpf.org.uk, accessed January 10, 2023. See also: Catia Cecilia Confortini, *Intelligent Feminist Critical Methodology in the Women's International League for Peace and Freedom* (London: Oxford University Press, 2012).

136. Leymah Gbowee was awarded the Nobel Peace Prize for her leadership of the Liberian non-violent women's peace movement, whose persistent activism compelled the dictator Charles Taylor and his rival male warlords to join peace negotiations in 1999. The building and sustaining of this inter-communal Liberian women's peace movement is the topic of the documentary film *Pray the Devil Back to Hell*, directed by Gini Reticker and produced by Abigail Disney (New York: Fork Films, 2008).

137. Bibiana Tanda, Tove Ivergård, Marie Sjöberg and Sylvie Ndongmo, *Global Feminist Cooperations During a Pandemic* (Geneva: WILPF, 2021).

138. I am deeply grateful to Elin Liss, a long-time WILPF-Sweden activist and officer, for tutoring me and including me in numerous Swedish feminist conversations and conferences.

139. See, for instance, the transnational feminist peace organization MADRE's new monthly newsletter, *Feminist Foreign Policy Memo* on www.madre.org, February 2023, accessed February 9, 2023.

140. Margot Wallström, "Without Women's Voices, Democracy and Peace are Weaker" in *The World Today*, February 3, 2023.

141. Eirinn Larsen, Sigrun Marie Moss and Inger Skjelsbæk, eds, *Gender Equality and Nation Branding in the Nordic Region* (London: Routledge, 2021).

142. Madeleine Rees, Secretary General of WILPF, based in Geneva, and Ray Acheson, head of WILPF's New York office's disarmament project, Reaching Critical Will, have been wonderfully generous in tutoring me on how feminist civil-society groups lobby the United Nations.

143. I'm grateful to Felicity Ruby for sharing her memories of this occasion with me.

144. I am especially grateful to Adriana Benjumea and Carla Afonso of Humanas Colombia, and Katherine Ronderos of WILPF-Colombia (Limpal-Colombia), as well as Laura Mitchell of NOREF, Oslo, for including me in this Bogotá conversation. See: Roxanne Krystalli and Kimberly Theidon, "Here's How Attention to Gender Affected Colombia's Peace Process" on *Washington Post,* October 9, 2016: www. washingtonpost.com/news/monkey-cage/wp/2016/10/09/heres-how-attention-to-gender-affected-colombias-peace-process

145. French feminist and long-time gender consultant to international agencies operating in war zones, Nadine Puechguirbal, has detailed how UN peacekeeping officials deployed to Haiti systematically ignored the information provided by local Haitian women activists: "Failing to Secure the Peace: A Conversation with Nadine Puechguirbal" in Chapter 7, in Cynthia Enloe, *Seriously! Investigating Crashes and Crises as If Women Mattered* (Berkeley: University of California Press, 2013, pp.124–150). For an account of how international policy-makers marginalized Syrian women peace activists in negotiations to end the war in Syria: Cynthia Enloe, "Syrian Women Resist Peace Table Patriarchy" in *The Big Push: Exposing and Challenging Persistent Patriarchy* (Brighton, UK: Myriad Editions; Berkeley: University of California Press, 2017, pp.24–47).

146. Joy Onyesoh, Madeleine Rees and Catia Cecilia Confortini, "Feminist Challenges to the Cooptation of WPS" in Soumita Basu, Paul Kirby and Laura Shepherd, eds, *New Directions in Women, Peace and Security* (Bristol, UK: Bristol University Press, 2020, pp.235–68). See also: Helen Kezie-Nwoha, Nela Porobić Isaković, Madeleine Rees and Sarah Smith, "Building and Conceptualizing Peace" in Sarah Smith and Keina Yoshida, eds, *Feminist Conversations on Peace* (Bristol, UK: Bristol University Press, 2022, pp.107–20).

Chapter Nine: "Post-war" Can Last Generations

147. The Associated Press, "As Kuwait Cracks Down, a Battle Erupts over Women's Rights" on National Public Radio, February 21, 2022: www.npt.org, accessed January 15, 2023. See also: Kim Murphy, "Kuwait Women Resist Iraq, Seek Recognition of Role" on *Los Angeles Times*, October 16, 1990: www.latimes.com, accessed January 16, 2023. Zeynep N. Kaya, "Have Efforts for Women's Political Participation in Kuwait Failed?" on London School of Economics (LSE), June 24, 2021: blogs.lse.ac.uk, accessed January 16, 2023. For regularly updated worldwide figures on women as the percentage of their own country's elected legislatures, see: Inter Parliamentary Union: www.ipu.org.

148. For a cross-national comparison of women's suffrage movements, including the Japanese suffrage movement, see: Caroline Daley and Melanie Nolan, eds, *Suffrage and Beyond: International Feminist Perspectives* (New York: New York University Press, 1994). For insights into Turkish (including Ottoman-era) feminist history: Zehra F Arat, "Kemalism and Turkish Women" in *Women and Politics*, vol. 14, no. 4, 1994, pp.57–80; Serpil Çakir, "Feminism and Feminist History-Writing

in Turkey" in *Aspasia*, vol. 1, no. 1, March 2007: www.berghahnjournals. com/view/journals/aspasia/1/1/asp010104.xml, accessed January 17, 2023. The most rigorously gathered comparative data on when, country by country, women won national voting rights on the same terms as men, see both: Joni Seager, *The Women's Atlas* (Brighton: Myriad Editions, 2018; New York: Penguin Books, 2018); Joni Seager, *The Penguin Atlas of Women in the World*, fourth edition (New York and London: Penguin, 2009).

149. In 2023, a South Korean judge for the first time held a South Korean military unit, the Second Marine Brigade, responsible for the massacre of South Vietnamese civilians – mainly children and women – in the villages of Phong Nhi and Phong Nhat, in central Vietnam. The plaintiff was Nguyen Thi Thanh, sixty-two. She was one of the survivors of the mass killing. The South Korean soldiers were deployed to South Vietnam as part of the US-led war operation. Of all the brutalities of that war, until this ruling, only one soldier – the American Lieutenant William Calley – had been convicted for mass killing in the Vietnam War. President Richard Nixon reduced Lt Calley's sentence from life imprisonment to several years of house arrest. Choe Sang-Hun, "South Korea Told to Pay a Vietnam War Victim" in *New York Times,* February 8, 2023.

150. A feminist-informed study of masculinities during and after war in Zimbabwe is: Jane Parpart, "Militarized Masculinities, Heroes and Gender Inequality During and After the Nationalist Struggle in Zimbabwe" in *NORMA: International Journal for Masculinity Studies,* vol. 10, issue 3–4, 2015, pp.312–25: www.tandfonline.com/doi/abs/10.10 80/18902138.2015.1110434, accessed January 15, 2023.

151. Leena Vastapuu, *Liberia's Women Veterans* (London: Zed Books, 2018, p.209). Vastapuu gives credit to another feminist researcher for helping her to see how and why post-war programs were designed in ways that left Liberian girls and women on society's post-war sidelines: Kathleen Jennings, "The Political Economy of DDR in Liberia: A Gendered Critique" in *Conflict, Security and Development,* vol. 9, no. 4, 2009, pp.475–94. For a valuable analysis of how Canadian women veterans' needs are neglected, see: Maya Eichler, "Making Military and Veteran Women (In)visible" in *Journal of Military Veteran and Family Health,* vol. 8, issue 1, April 2022, pp.36–45.

152. Leena Vastapuu, "Beans, Bullets and Bandages? Gendering Combat Service Support," forthcoming.

153. One of the first feminist researchers to write about the masculinizing gun requirement in the DDR system was the South African feminist gender consultant, Vanessa Farr. See, for instance: Vanessa Farr, "The

Importance of a Gender Perspective to Successful Disarmament, Demobilization and Reintegration Processes," *Disarmament Forum,* no. 4, 2003, pp.25–36. Also eye opening is: Susan McKay and Dyan Mazurana, *Where Are the Girls? Girls in Fighting Forces in Northern Uganda, Sierra Leone and Mozambique: Their Lives During and After War,* (Montreal: Rights and Democracy, 2004). Additional insights into women veterans' post-war struggles are provided by: Megan H. MacKenzie, *Female Soldiers in Sierra Leone: Sex, Security and Post-Conflict Development,* (New York, NYU Press, 2012).

154. Oretha in conversation with Leena Vastapuu, "Beans, Bullets and Bandages," forthcoming. Leena Vastapuu is a professor in the Gender and War Program at the Swedish University of Defense, Stockholm.

155. A moving triple biography of three American World War II male veterans, whose post-war silences cost them their mental health, is: Thomas Childers, *Soldier from the War Returning* (Boston: Houghton Mifflin Harcourt, 2009).

156. Theresa De Langis, a feminist human-rights researcher, spent years documenting the sexually abusive realities lived by Cambodian women forced into marriages by the Khmer Rouge: Theresa De Langis, *Like Ghost Changes Body: Interviews on the Impact of Forced Marriage During the Khmer Rouge Regime* (Phnom Penh: Transcultural Psychosocial Organization Cambodia, 2015). Theresa De Langis is one of those named on the Gender Justice Legacy Wall in The Hague. Feminist scholar Elora Halim Chowdhury explores the silences surrounding Bangladeshi women's wartime experiences of rape – and the post-war telling of those stories only decades later – in: Elora Halim Chowdhury, *Ethical Encounters: Transnational Feminism, Human Rights, and War Cinema in Bangladesh* (Philadelphia: Temple University Press, 2022).

157. Ayşe Gül Altinay and Andrea Petö, eds, *Gendered Wars, Gendered Memories* (London and New York: Routledge, 2016).

158. See Elizabeth D Samet, *Looking for the Good War: American Amnesia and the Violent Pursuit of Happiness* (New York: Farrar, Straus and Giroux, 2021). A fresh historical account of Germany's post-war era that gives careful attention to women's experiences is: Harald Jahner, *Life in the Fallout of the Third Reich, 1945–1955* (New York: Knopf, 2021).

159. Monument to the Women of World War II: www.iwm.org.uk/memorials/item/memorial/51288. For a feminist analysis of recent British war monuments within a cross-country comparison, see: Vron Ware, "The New National War Monuments" in Cecilia Ase and Maria Wendt, eds, *Gendering Military Sacrifice: A Feminist Comparative Analysis* (London and New York: Routledge, 2019, pp.68–95). See

also: Birgitte Refslund Sørensen, "Public Commemorations of Danish Soldiers: Monuments, Memorials, and Tombstones" in *Critical Military Studies,* vol. 3, no. 1, April 2017, pp.27–49; Cecilia Ase, "Rationalizing Military Death: The Politics of the New Military Monuments in Berlin and Stockholm" in *Critical Military Studies,* vol. 8, no. 1, March 2022, pp.77–98.

160. Vietnam Women's Memorial: www.vietnamwomensmemorial.org /history.php

161. Gender Justice Legacy Wall: 4genderjustice.org/gender-justice-legacy-wall-2. I am happily indebted to the late Rita Arditti, an Argentinian feminist researcher, who insisted that I think seriously about the gendered politics of impunity: Rita Arditti, *Searching for Life: The Grandmothers of the Plaza de Mayo* (Berkeley: University of California Press, 1999).

162. The Srebrenica Museum: galerija110795.ba. The museum is part of the International Coalition of Sites of Conscience.

163. Manzanar National Historic Site: www.nps.gov/manz/index.htm. Among the memoirs by Japanese Americans detained at Manzanar is: James D Houston and Jeanne Wakatsuki Houston, *Farewell to Manzanar* (Boston: Houghton and Mifflin, 1973). For a historical account of the US government's detention of Italian Americans without trial during World War II: David A Taylor, "During World War II, the U.S. Saw Italian-Americans as a Threat to Homeland Security" in *Smithsonian Magazine,* February 2017. During World War II, the British government interned on the Isle of Man 12,000 German and Austrian refugees – most of them Jewish – without trial: Simon Parkin, *The Island of Extraordinary Captives: A Painter, a Poet, an Heiress, and a Spy in a World War II British Internment Camp* (New York: Scribner, 2022).

164. Rosie the Riveter World War II National Historical Site: nps.gov/rori/ index.htm. A documentary film featuring white and African American women who worked in (and later were laid off from) World War II defense plants is: Connie Field, director, Connie Field producer, *The Life and Times of Rosie the Riveter* (Clarity Films, 1980).

165. Women's Active Museum on War and Peace: www.wam-peace.org. When I visited the museum in 2013, accompanied by Japanese feminist scholar Fumiko Sato, I was shown around the museum and given a sense of its carefully tended relationships with women survivors by the then director Mina Watanabe. Among Watanabe's writings is: Mina Watanabe, "Passing on the History of 'Comfort Women': The Experience of a Woman's Museum in Japan" in *Journal of Peace Education,* vol. 12, np. 3, 2015. I am grateful to Professor Ruri Ito for

introducing me to so many Japanese anti-militarist feminists, including Mina Watanabe.

166. Naomi Klein, *The Shock Doctrine* (New York: Macmillan, 2007). South Sudanese women activists greeted Pope Francis's visit in 2023 because he shone a light on the corrupt alliance between local post-war South Sudanese elite men and the male executives of exploitative foreign mining companies, who in turn hired militarized private security companies: Declan Walsh and Jason Horowitz, "In South Sudan, Pope Recounts Troubles of Young, Fractured Nation" in *New York Times*, February 4, 2023.

167. Among the feminist transnational scholars who have devoted years to bringing together researchers and activists to hammer out reconstruction alternatives is University of Massachusetts-Boston professor Carol Cohn. She and her colleagues call their project "A Feminist Roadmap for Sustainable Peace."

168. Gorana Mlinarević and Nela Porobić, *The Peace That is Not* (Geneva: Women's International League for Peace and Freedom, 2021).

169. A detailed account of how sex-trafficking operated – and was officially ignored – in post-war Bosnia is provided by the American woman police officer who uncovered and made public the abusive system: Kathryn Bolkovac, with Cari Lynn, *The Whistleblower* (London: Palgrave, 2011). Kathryn Bolkovac is among those named on the Gender Justice Legacy Wall in The Hague.

170. Mlinarević and Porobić, *The Peace That is Not* (p.14). A prescient collection of analyses of Dayton's militarized, gender-uninformed deliberations and their consequences is: Cynthia Cockburn and Dubravka Zarkov, eds, *The Postwar Moment: Militaries, Masculinities and International Peacekeeping* (London: Lawrence and Wishart, 2002).

Chapter Ten: Militarization Starts during Peacetime

171. Joni Seager, in conversation with the author, Cambridge, MA, October, 2022.

172. Joni Seager, *Working Towards Gender Equality in the Ranger Workforce* on Universal Ranger Support Alliance (URSA), 2021: www.ursa4rangers. org. Seager, a feminist environmental expert, is a gender consultant to the World Wildlife Fund.

173. For an analysis of the US Defense Department's new intimacy with many American research universities, funding joint artificial intelligence weapons research projects: Michael T Klare, "The Pentagon's Quest for Academic Intelligence: Remilitarizing the University" on *The Nation,* February 2023, www.thenation.com, accessed February 2,

2023. A detailed account of the Egyptian military's current control of the country's economy through vast military enterprises and companies owned by former military officers – and the International Monetary Fund's efforts to shrink the Egyptian military's business holdings – is: Vivian Yee, "Egypt's Economy Buckles Under Punishing Inflation" in *New York Times*, January 24, 2023. Many women active in Syria's Arab Spring pro-democracy movement were reluctant to respond to the Assad regime's violent crackdown with a male-led anti-government armed opposition: Samar Yazbek, *A Woman in the Crossfire: Diaries of the Syrian Revolution* (London: Haus Publishing, 2012). Korean feminist researcher and activist Insook Kwon has candidly tracked the militarization of her country's pro-democracy movement during its 1980s protests, in which she took part: Insook Kwon, "How Identities and Movement Culture Became Deeply Saturated with Militarism: Lessons from the Pro-Democracy Movement of South Korea" in *Asian Journal of Women's Studies,* vol. 11, issue 2, 1995, pp.7–40. A feminist-informed account of the processes that have imbued many South Koreans with a militarized world view is: Nora Kim and Seungsook Moon, "Transnational Militarism and Ethnic Nationalism: South Korean Involvements in the Vietnam and Iraq Wars" in *Critical Military Studies,* vol. 8, no. 4, 2022, pp.409–27.

174. Widely read among these investigations of women attracted to 1920s-30s militarized fascism is Claudia Koonz, *Mothers in the Fatherland* (New York: St Martin's Press, 1986). On women attracted to Italian fascism: Victoria De Grazia, *How Fascism Ruled Women: Italy 1922–1945* (Berkeley: University of California Press, 1992). A cross-national study of European fascist women, giving special attention to British women who joined fascist groups in the 1930s, is: Martin Durham, *Women and Fascism* (London: Routledge, 1998).

175. Ximena Bunster, "Watch Out for the Little Nazi Man That All of Us Have Inside: The Mobilization and Demobilization of Women in Militarized Chile" in *Women's Studies International Forum,* vol. 11, no. 5, 1988, pp.485–91; Margaret Power, *Right-wing Women in Chile* (State College, PA: Penn State University Press, 2002).

176. The Romanian political scientist Professor Liliana Popescu, has responded to the patriarchal stereotype of women as "too emotional" to analyze national security and foreign policy by creating the innovative network of south-eastern and Eastern European women national security experts: ESEE FANEL: www.esee-fanel.net.

177. I am grateful to dozens of Fellows who, over twelve years, have taken part in the University of Iceland's Gender Equality Studies Program (GEST) for helping me think through these ideas. The lived experiences

of these mid-career civil servants and NGO staff – in Kenya, Malawi, Mozambique, Ghana, Uganda, Pakistan, Palestine, Afghanistan, Kosovo, Serbia, Russia, Sri Lanka, Mexico and China – made the people holding these ideas appear the complex individuals they are. Irma Erlingsdóttir, Giti Chandra, Annadís Rúdólfsdóttir, Gudrún Eysteinsdóttir and the wonderful staff of the GEST program gave me the opportunity to engage with these thoughtful Fellows.

178. Gun Free Kitchen Tables: www.gfkt.org. GFKT is part of a transnational alliance in which many women are locally active, International Action Network on Small Arms: www.iansa.org. Rela Mazali, one of the feminist founders of GFKT, has taught me about Israeli feminists' ever-evolving anti-militarism strategies.

179. Women Cross DMZ, Christine Ahn, Executive Director: www.womencrossdmz.org.

180. A remarkably detailed first-hand account of the women-led ICAN campaign's alliance-building and strategizing is: Ray Acheson, *Banning the Bomb, Smashing the Patriarchy* (Lanham, MD: Rowman & Littlefield, 2021). Continuing the feminist-informed research on nuclear weapons, with attention on the Pacific, is Catherine Eschle's and Shine Choi's project "Rethinking Nuclear Politics" at Strathclyde University, Scotland.

181. The late Cynthia Cockburn was among the most visible members of the internationally loosely networked Women in Black. The British Library interviewed her about the origins and goals of Women in Black: www.bl.uk/collection-items/cynthia-cockburn-women-in-black. I am indebted to Lepa Mladjenovic, Ruri Ito, Rela Mazali and Cynthia Cockburn for introducing me to Women in Black local activists. Another group of women who disrupted traffic to non-violently protest their government's shrinkage of national belonging is India's 2019–21 Shaheen Bagh movement: Amrita Basu and Anna Pathan, "The Revolution Will Come Wearing Bangles, Bindis and Hijabs: Women's Activism for Inclusive Citizenship" in Chapter 10, Amrita Basu and Anna Pathan, eds, *Women, Gender and Religious Nationalism* (Cambridge, UK: Cambridge University Press, 2022).

182. For first-hand accounts by women who demonstrated at Greenham Common: Alice Cook and Gwyn Kirk, *Greenham Women Everywhere: Dreams, Ideas and Actions from the Women's Peace Movement* (London: Pluto Press, 1983; Boston: South End Press, 1983). See also: Catherine Eschle and Alison Bartlett, eds: *Feminism and Protest Camps*, (Bristol: Bristol University Press, 2023). My long-time friend Margaret Bluman has described to me the importance to herself and hundreds of other British women of becoming a "Greenham woman" in the 1980s. David

Vine has used his anthropological skills to investigate scores of US military bases around the world, how local civilians view those bases, and how the US government (the Pentagon and Congress) have justified those bases: David Vine, *Base Nation: How U.S. Military Bases Abroad Harm America and the World* (New York: Metropolitan Books, 2015). A thoroughly historicized and intersectional study of a single US military base, Fort Bragg, and its host town, Fayetteville, North Carolina, is: Catherine Lutz, *Home Front: A Military City and the American Twentieth Century* (Boston: Beacon Press, 2022). A history of West Indians who worked as civilians on the US base in Guantánamo, Cuba, during the Cold War is: Jana Lipman, *Guantánamo: A Working-Class History Between Empire and Revolution* (Berkeley: University of California Press, 2009). Among the studies of civilians who have changed their minds – their ideas – about the benefits of living near a military base is: Joni Seager, *Earth Follies* (New York: Routledge, 2006); Catherine Lutz, ed., *The Bases of Empire: The Global Struggle Against U.S. Military Posts* (London: Pluto Press, 2009). My own exploration of the gender politics that shape the lives of diverse women living on and near military bases is: Cynthia Enloe, *Bananas, Beaches and Bases,* second edition (Berkeley: University of California Press, 2014).

183. Suzuyo Takazato, leader of Okinawan Women Act Against Military Violence, generously tutored me on the anti-bases movement and why women have been so crucial to sustaining it, despite opposition from both Tokyo and Washington policy-makers. Suzuyo also gave me a guided tour of the US bases, which occupy so much of Okinawa's arable land. For the experiences of Okinawan women civilians working on US bases: Nora Weinek and Fumika Sato, "Living with U.S. Forces in Okinawa, Japan: The Ambivalent Experiences of Women Working on Base" in *Journal of Gender Studies,* Hitotsubashi University, July, 2019, pp.93–110. (This paper is published in Japanese, though Fumika Sato sent me a draft version in English). Gabriela is the Filipina feminist network that did so much to expose the negative impacts on Filipinos of the enormous US Navy base at Subic Bay. Filipina novelist Gina Apostol on the flawed reasoning behind the proposal to create new US military bases in the Philippines: Gina Apostol, "The Curse of the Philippines' Geography" in *New York Times,* February 8, 2023. A gender- and racism-aware ethnographic study of local civilians living with and working for the US missile-launching base on Kwajalein Atoll in the Marshall Islands is: Lauren Hirshberg, *Suburban Empire: Cold War Militarization in the US Pacific* (Berkeley: University of California Press, 2022).

184. Gabriel Dominguez, "Recruitment Issues Undermining Japan's Military Buildup" on *Japan Times,* January 2, 2023: www.japantimes.co.jp/

news/2023/01/02/national/japan-sdf-recruitment-problems, accessed January 30, 2023.

185. A collection of anthropologists' analyses of militarization is: Roberto J González, Hugh Gusterson and Gustaaf Houtman, eds, *Militarization: A Reader* (Durham, NC: Duke University Press, 2019). Hugh Gusterson's unusual ethnography tracking the militarization of civilian men and women working as scientists and technicians at a California nuclear weapons laboratory is: Hugh Gusterson, *Nuclear Rites: A Weapons Laboratory at the End of the Cold War* (Berkeley: University of California Press, 1996).

186. Cynthia Cockburn, *From Where We Stand: War, Women's Activism and Feminist Analysis* (London: Zed Books, 2007). The late Cynthia Cockburn based this book on interviews with anti-militarization feminist activists in Sierra Leone, India, Colombia, Palestine, Serbia, Israel and Turkey. The local activists themselves often networked internationally with each other through Women in Black and WILPF.

187. Virginia Woolf, *A Room of One's Own* (London: Penguin Books, 2004, p.44). *A Room of One's Own* was originally published in 1929 by Hogarth Press, a publishing company created by Virginia and Leonard Woolf. A description of Woolf's *Dreadnought* caper is in Hermione Lee, *Virginia Woolf* (London: Vintage, 1997). Almost simultaneously, Woolf was writing *Mrs Dalloway,* her most famous novel, portraying two British post-war distraught lives. A wonderfully eye-opening annotated new edition of *Mrs Dalloway* is: Virginia Woolf, *The Annotated Mrs. Dalloway,* edited by Merve Emre (New York: W W Norton, 2021). Also valuable is Karen L Levenback, *Virginia Woolf and the Great War* (Syracuse, NY: Syracuse University Press, 1999). I am grateful to Eve Lacey, Librarian of Newnham College, Cambridge University, for showing me around Newnham College in October and November 2022 and telling me of its suffrage history.

188. The edition of Woolf's famous anti-militarism book that includes her own original photographs of professional men in their elaborate attire, as well as excerpts from her contemporaneous letters and diaries, is: Virginia Woolf, *Three Guineas,* annotated by Jane Marcus (New York: Harcourt, Inc., 2006). It was my friend Serena Hilsinger, a Woolf scholar, who first pushed me to read – and teach – *Three Guineas.*

189. A major project in rethinking the so-called canon of international political thinking has been launched by four British feminist scholars: Patricia Owens, Katharina Rietzler, Kimberly Hutchings and Sarah C Dunstan. Their publications thus far: Patricia Owens, Katharina Rietzler, Kimberly Hutchings and Sarah C Dunstan, eds, *Women's International Thought: Towards a New Canon* (Cambridge, UK:

Cambridge University Press, 2022); Patricia Owens and Katharina Rietzler, eds, *Women's International Thought: A New History* (Cambridge, UK: Cambridge University Press, 2020). As these scholars note, this is just a beginning. The women thinkers featured so far are from North America and Western Europe. That, of course, is incomplete. Turkish, Egyptian, Chinese, Indian, Japanese, Hawaiian and Nigerian women of the pre-1950s eras were thinking about international politics. We need to learn from them. A recent historical account of how women in the early twentieth century put then current feminist ideas into transnational practice – at the Versailles peace negotiations and in Geneva at the new League of Nations – is: Mona L Siegel, *Peace on Our Terms: The Global Battle for Women's Rights After the First World War* (New York: Columbia University Press, 2020). My own belated effort to give credit to an overlooked woman international thinker, one of my undergraduate teachers, is: Cynthia Enloe, "On Whose Shoulders Am I Standing? My Debt to Louise Holborn" in a special "Forum: Theorizing the History of Women's International Thinking at the 'End of International Theory'" in Adom Getachew, Duncan Bell, Cynthia Enloe and Vineet Thakur, eds, *International Theory,* vol. 14, no. 3, October 2022, pp.1–25.

Chapter Eleven: Ukrainian Feminists Have Lessons to Teach Us about War

190. This Odesa meeting was co-hosted in 2018 by the Swedish international feminist development organization Kvinna till Kvinna (Women to Women) and the Women's International League for Peace and Freedom (WILPF). Both groups had projects in Ukraine.
191. Martha Bohachevsky-Chomiak, "Women's Movement" in Danylo Husar Struk, ed., *Encyclopedia of Ukraine* (Toronto: University of Toronto Press, 1993 edition): www.encyclopediaofukraine.com, accessed January 30, 2023.
192. Olga Plakhotnik, in conversation with the author, Greifswald, Germany, August, 2022.
193. Roxanna Carrillo, Charlotte Bunch and Anne Marie Goetz were among the feminists who strategized to create UN Women. The predecessor of UN Women was UNIFEM, an agency within the large UN Development Program (UNDP). Though many of UNIFEM's staff were feminists with gender expertise, the promoters of UN Women hoped that taking the agency dedicated to women's rights and development out from under another large department and placing it up

on a level with other large UN entities would give its director – and thus its commitments to women's equality and well-being – direct access to the UN Secretary General.

194. Merit Hietanen, Oksana Potapova, Christina Haneef, Ganna Kvit and Felicia Dahlquist, *Rapid Gender Analysis of Ukraine* (New York: UN Women and CARE, May 2022). A documentary film tracking six of the Ukrainian women who began volunteering for the Ukrainian military in 2014, in order to make visible women's military contributions, is Maria Berlinska, producer, *Invisible Battalion*, 2018: invisiblebattalion.org.

195. Oksana Potapova quoted in: "In the Words of Oksana Potapova: 'We Need Radical Transformation'" on UN Women, May 29, 2019: www.unwomen.org/news/stories/2019/5/in-the-words-of-oksana-potapova, accessed January 31, 2023.

196. Trisha de Borchgrave, "Ukraine Needs Women to Win the War – and the Peace" on *World Today,* Chatham House, February 3, 2023: www.chathamhouse.org/publications/the-world-today/2023-02/ukraine-needs-women-win-war-and-peace, accessed February 6, 2023.

197. The economic data here are from UN Women, Merit Hietanen, Oksana Potapova, Christina Haneef, Ganna Kvit and Felicia Dahlquist, *Rapid Gender Analysis of Ukraine,* p.14.

198. Ibid., p.16.

199. Yeva Skalietska, *You Don't Know What War Is: The Diary of a Young Girl from Ukraine* (London: Bloomsbury, 2022).

200. Merit Hietanen, Oksana Potapova, Christina Haneef, Ganna Kvit and Felicia Dahlquist, *Rapid Gender Analysis of Ukraine,* p.14.

201. Ibid., interviewees quoted, p.20.

202. Oksana Potapova, in conversation with the author, Greifswald, Germany, July, 2022.

203. Interviews with Nina Potarska: "Ukrainian Peace Activist: My Country Has Become a Battlefield for Major Powers. End the War Now" on *Democracy Now,* February 25, 2022: www.democracynow.org/2022/2/25/ukrainian_peace_activist, accessed February 2, 2023; "The Peace Activist: 'Our Lives Will Never Be As Before'", Kvinna till Kvinna, April 27, 2022: www.kvinnatillkvinna.org/2022/04/27/the-peace-activist-our-lives, accessed February 1, 2023. For WILPF's analysis, see: Madeleine Rees, "War 'Over' Ukraine – Militarism is Killing Us ALL, Writes WILPF Secretary-General in an Open Letter to the UNSC" on WILPF, January 2022: www.wilpf.org, accessed February 2, 2023.

204. Nina Potarska, interview with Kvinna till Kvinna, April 27, 2022: www.kvinnatillkvinna.org/2022/04/27/the-peace-activist-our-lives-will-never-be-as-before, accessed February 1, 2023.

205. Nina Potarska, quoted in "Democracy Now," February 25, 2022.

206. I am grateful to Maria Mayerchyk and Olga Plakhotnik for inviting me to take part in their "Thinking Under Bombing" summer school in Greifswald, Germany in August 2022. They continue to be researchers on the faculty of the University of Greifswald.

207. See, for instance, Hannah Arendt, *Thinking Without a Banister* (New York: Schocken Books, 2018).

208. One of Ukraine's feminist civil-society groups working to establish the rule of law is Women Lawyers of Ukraine (JurFem): Hrystyna Kit, "Helping Ukraine's Sex-Crime Survivors" on *World Today*, Chatham House, February 3, 2023: www.chathamhouse.org, accessed February 3, 2023. The memoir by an American woman ambassador to Ukraine who advocated for the rule of law in the crucial years after the Russian conquest of Crimea, and who resisted the Trump administration's questionable attempts to gain influence with the Ukrainian government, is: Marie Yovanovitch, *Lessons from the Edge: A Memoir* (New York: Mariner Books, 2022).

209. Regarding efforts to create new citizen-friendly police in Ukraine: Marc Santora, "Drunks and Drones: Life as a Cop in Kyiv" in *New York Times,* February 10, 2023.

210. A graphic account of Ukraine's Revolution of Dignity, based on interviews with participants, is: Marci Shore, *The Ukrainian Night: An Intimate History of Revolution* (New Haven, CT: Yale University Press, 2017).

211. Women's Perspectives Center, "Submission of Information on Femicide" in Lviv, 2021: www.women.lviv.ua, accessed Feb 2, 2023.

212. United Nations Special Rapporteur on Violence Against Women: www.ohchr.org. The first person appointed to the post of Special Rapporteur was Radhika Coomaraswamy. For her work, Coomaraswamy has been named on the Wall of Gender Justice at the ICC in The Hague.

213. Merit Hietanen, Oksana Potapova, Christina Haneef, Ganna Kvit and Felicia Dahlquist, *Rapid Gender Analysis of Ukraine,* p.39.

214. Ukrainian sex workers reported that, once the war began, more of their Ukrainian male clients had guns. That made the sex workers wary. Their armed male clients were more likely to refuse to pay the women's established rates and more likely to demand additional services from them for free. Social workers who had spent years building trust with sex workers reported that the war made it harder to stay in contact with women needing support to handle drug addiction and HIV. Prostitution is not legal in Ukraine, but it is widely tolerated. Prior to 2022, men from other European countries had traveled to Ukraine for sex tourism. Those male clients, sex workers

report, have disappeared in wartime: Maria Varenikova, "Juggling Sex, Secrecy and Safety as Battles Rage All Around" in *New York Times*, January 31, 2023.

215. Yaryna Grusha Possamai, "Kyiv's Continuing Failure to Implement the Istanbul Convention" on Kennan Institute, Wilson Center, July 13, 2020: www.wilsoncenter.org/blog-post/kyivs-continuing-failure-implement-istanbul-convention, accessed Feb 3, 2023.

216. Iryna Slavinska, "'Historic Victory for Women's Rights': Ukraine Ratifies Istanbul Convention", Ukraine Alert on Atlantic Council, June 21, 2022: www.atlanticcouncil.org/ukrainealert/historic-victory-for-womens-rights, accessed February 3, 2023.

217. Marta Chumalo quoted in "An Activist from Ukraine Received the Swedish Prize in the Field of Human Rights Protection" on *Odessa Journal*, January 10, 2023: www.odessa-journal.com. See also: www.palmefonden.se.

Acknowledgments

HOW DO THEY DO IT? Really, how do they keep their eyes wide open to the horrors of war and meanness of misogyny yet still find the spirit to listen, laugh and lend their stories and knowledge to the rest of us? I'm talking, of course, about feminist peace activists. Feminist activists think, question, investigate. They bring women together. They insist on gender-revealing data. They hold institutions and movements accountable. Feminist activists make all of us smarter about this complex, dynamic, interconnected world.

The feminist advocates and peace activists who especially have informed this book are: the late Cynthia Cockburn, Madeleine Rees, Ray Acheson, Rela Mazali, Insook Kwon, Christine Chinkin, Elin Liss, Christine Ahn, Charlotte Bunch, Roxanna Carrillo, the late-Rita Arditti, Cynthia Rothschild, Marie-Aimée Hélie-Lucas, Nadine Puechguirbal, Lepa Mladjenović, Nela Porobić Isaković, Gorana Mlinarević, Agnes Gund, Abigail Disney, the late Jean Hardesty, Tanya Henderson, Ristin Thomasson, Nebahat Akkoc, Mikaela Luttrell-Rowland, Adriana Benjumea, Carla Afonso, Katherine Roderos, Ngoc Du Thai Thi, Purna Sen, Vanessa Farr, Petra Totterman Andorff, Lory Manning, Carolyn Becraft, Edwin Dorn, Phoebe Donnelly, Theresa de Langis and Sohaila Abdulali.

Feminist teacher/scholars. No false binaries here. To teach is to listen and stay curious. To conduct research is to enliven teaching. Commitments to feminist-informed social justice make one's teaching and research more nuanced, reliable and valuable. Do read all the Notes here. Every note is a personal thank you. I am so grateful for the careful work each of these scholar/teachers is doing.

Ukrainian feminists are doing everything, all at once, during wartime's dangers and displacements. Their names should be on all our lips. Their understandings should be guiding our actions. No discussion of Ukraine's present or future should be without them prominently at the table. Among those Ukrainian feminists who have been opening my mind are Olga Plakhotnik, Maria Mayerchyk, Marta Chumalo, Nina Potarska and Oksana Potapova.

Universities are made more intellectually valuable by their scholarly innovators. During the initial months of writing this book, I was welcomed and inspired by colleagues and post-graduate students at the Cambridge University Centre for Gender Studies, especially Lauren Wilcox, Holly Porter, Jude Browne, Laura Bush and Vincenzo Paci. With special thanks to the generous donors who support the Centre and the Diane Middlebrook and Carl Djerassi Visiting Professorship.

No feminist book sees the light of day in handsome, readable form without the skills, commitments and hard professional work of editors and their publishing colleagues. Footnote Press and the University of California Press are every author's dream teams. Candida Lacey, a decades-long friend, has been central to this project from its very beginning. Over coffee and wine, in cafes and on Zoom, she has offered her publishing and political wisdom. Vidisha Biswas is the creator of the wonderfully fresh Footnote Press. I am so lucky to be a small part of their innovative publishing venture. Naomi Schneider, Executive Editor of the University of California Press, has been, as she always is, an inspiration. To Fritha Saunders, Vicki Heath Silk, the external reviewers and the skilled production and marketing teams at both Footnote and UCal Press I owe warm thanks.

Joni Seager is the absolutely best of partners. She keeps me on my toes. She generously shares her amazing wealth of feminist knowledge. Even in the darkest of times, her irreverence keeps the laughter flowing.

Index

About the author

Cynthia Enloe is a feminist activist, researcher and teacher. She is Research Professor at Clark University in Massachusetts and internationally known for her work on women and militarism, in the global garment, banana, diplomatic and banking industries, and in domestic service.

Her fifteen books, including *Bananas, Beaches and Bases: Making Feminist Sense of International Politics*, have been translated into Chinese, French, Icelandic, Japanese, Spanish, Swedish, Turkish and Ukrainian. She has been awarded honorary doctorates from universities around the world and regularly appears on international news channels.

In 2018, Cynthia Enloe was chosen as one of the 100 names written on the Gender Justice Wall at the International Criminal Court in The Hague.